Places, Please!

Becoming a Jersey Boy

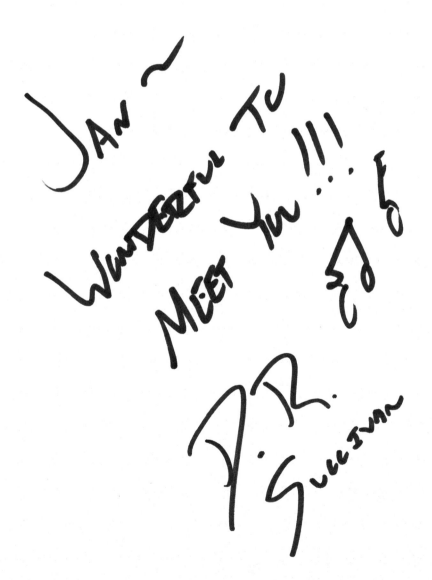

Jan ~
Wonderful to
Meet you !!! ...
P. R. Sullivan

Places, Please!
Becoming a Jersey Boy

Daniel Robert Sullivan

IGUANA

Copyright © 2012 Daniel Robert Sullivan
Published by Iguana Books
460 Richmond St. West, Suite 401
Toronto, Ontario, Canada
M5V 1Y1

Publisher: Greg Ioannou
Editor: Lisa Sparks
Front cover image: Andres Alvez, www.andresalvez.com
Front cover design: Lea Kaplan
Book layout design: Sharlene Hopwood, Stephanie Martin

Sullivan, Daniel Robert
    Places, please! : Becoming a Jersey Boy / Daniel Robert Sullivan.

Issued also in electronic formats.
ISBN 978-0-9878267-2-5

    1. Sullivan, Daniel Robert. 2. Singers--United States--Biography.
I. Title.

ML420.S949A3 2012   782.1'4092   C2011-907116-9

This is the first revised print edition of *Places, Please!: Becoming a Jersey Boy.*

Contents

FOREWORD

I am very honored to be chosen by Daniel Robert Sullivan to introduce this new book describing his most fascinating, behind-the-scenes journey to becoming one of the leads in the smash production of *Jersey Boys* in Toronto, Canada.

I found that I could not put the book down. Daniel's personal story is tremendously inspiring — especially for anyone who wants to become an actor or member of the theatrical industry. I commend Daniel for having the foresight to keep a written journal documenting his experiences and feelings through the grueling audition process and on to becoming selected for his plum role; the type of role that comes around perhaps once or twice in a lifetime.

The honesty in his storytelling is most touching as we witness the personal sacrifices that he makes to be an actor, a profession that is usually more emotionally rewarding than it is financially. I love his passion for theatre. It is so earnest and simultaneously, slightly self-deprecating.

As the Canadian Producer of *Jersey Boys*, I had the pleasure of working with Daniel when my partner, Dodger Theatricals in New York, selected him to play the lead role of Tommy DeVito. I grew to know Daniel personally as a warm human being who truly loves life and his family. I would drop by his dressing room before the show on a regular basis. We became friends and Daniel would occasionally come over to my office — next door to the theatre — for coffee or lunch. We would talk about producing shows, as he always wanted to learn more about the business side of things.

After reading this book, my personal admiration increased significantly. His story provides a window into the many aspects of an actor's day-to-day life that I was not aware of or appreciated. I learned how challenging it is, and what it *really* takes to become an actor. There are more downs than ups, but when you've landed a lead role and you are performing on stage in a show like *Jersey Boys*, you find the ride well worth it.

In Toronto, long before Daniel was offered the role of Tommy DeVito, there was a theatre monopoly in the city that I felt could be challenged. The vacuum created with the demise of Garth Drabinsky's Livent, Inc. left the main stage of the Toronto Centre for the Arts virtually dark for ten years, with no Broadway shows, until Dancap Productions was created.

A decade ago, Toronto was ranked among the three most thrilling and vibrant live theatre cities on earth, not that far behind New York City and London. I got to know long-time producer Michael David, founder of Dodger Theatricals, through my experience with *Urinetown: The Musical* at Canadian Stage. Michael became my ally, partner, and friend in bringing *Jersey Boys* to Toronto. He, like myself, wanted to make a difference in the Toronto theatre landscape, believing that competition is good for the city and the country. Michael is in his late-sixties and his distinguished, yet bushy, beard makes him look like one of the guitar players from ZZ Top. He has more than a few battle scars from his years on Broadway and the wisdom of Noah. I was a producer who had no producing experience, yet I had the drive and good fortune to see his show become a huge success.

To compensate for my theatrical deficiencies, I put together a first-class team of very experienced people who had worked at Livent. Led by Peter Lamb, my executive vice president, I could not be in the business without this incredible team. They all have a sincere and continuing passion for the business of theatre and a strong desire to participate in the journey, opportunity, and adventure of bringing great theatre to the city of Toronto.

Everyone in the theatre crew at the Toronto Centre for the Arts — those in wardrobe, wigs, props, stage management, marketing, sales, the actors, the musicians — all had a singular goal in mind: to make *Jersey Boys* as successful as possible, while still having fun. The talent and the enthusiasm were off the charts! People not only loved their jobs, but their collaboration, performance after performance, was remarkable. It seemed life could not get any better. The relationships and bonds that were made, on and off the stage, will be everlasting. There was no visible hierarchy between the different positions, including mine. I was more than content to be one of the crew! We wanted to perform to the best of our ability and keep the show running as long as we could.

Each performance was unique; as was each audience, and we loved them all.. The entire company wanted to know, "What's the audience going to be like today? Are they going to be excited, happy, quiet?" Some came to see *Jersey Boys* more than a hundred times and seeing the show multiple times became a badge of honor. The actors would always take the time to meet with their superfans outside the stage door or connect with them on Facebook, because they knew that they were the people who helped keep the flame of *Jersey Boys* alive.

Then came the day in July 2010, when Michael David and I decided that, after one million people had seen *Jersey Boys*, we had reached the outer ring of what I call the concentric circle of theatregoers in Toronto and had to close the show on August 22nd, 2010, exactly two years after it opened. We both knew that American visitors were no longer coming to Toronto, a passport became required — 65% of Americans didn't have one — and the Canadian exchange rate was not as favorable as in the past.. Once we had made this decision and started to advertise the show was ending, all those that had been on the fence about seeing it started coming in droves.

The final performance of *Jersey Boys* in Toronto was like a reverse opening. We had a theatre full of dedicated *Jersey Boys* fans who knew all the lines of the show, were singing all the lyrics, and were going crazy throughout. The audience went absolutely insane and the standing ovation that night lasted ten minutes. It was the climax of reviving a dark theatre, restoring its purpose and glory, and indeed, having a profound effect on those that worked in it directly or indirectly — and especially those that attended.

Daniel Robert Sullivan is now in the history books of theatre in Toronto, having played the role of Tommy DeVito in *Jersey Boys*. The show holds the record for the longest running show at the Toronto Centre for the Arts, beating out mega-hits *Showboat, Ragtime,* and *Sunset Boulevard.* Daniel's dream, like mine, became a reality, which is now etched into our mind, body, and soul forever. What an amazing journey for all!

Aubrey Dan
President, Dancap Productions Inc.

PROLOGUE

Everyone's heard of *Jersey Boys*. Thirteen million people have seen the show, totaling more than $1 billion in worldwide ticket sales. The cast members have performed on *The Oprah Winfrey Show*, the *Today* show, *Dancing with the Stars*, and at the Emmy Awards. Their recording has gone Platinum, selling more than a million copies in the United States alone. There are six companies performing it around the world right now: New York, Las Vegas, London, Australia…the boys are everywhere.

My first experience with the production of *Jersey Boys* came via my then soon-to-be wife. Knowing my love for anything new on Broadway, Cara gave me tickets to the show for my birthday in March of 2007. We had lived together in New York for less than a year and, although we were both working, our budget still dictated we sit in the very back row of the August Wilson Theatre.

The performance of *Jersey Boys* that night was mind-bogglingly fast and endlessly passionate. The show just drives; taking the audience on a ride that culminates in a raucous standing ovation. (I've checked the show reports—every company of *Jersey Boys* around the world has received a standing ovation every single night since they opened.)

Jersey Boys tells the story of the Four Seasons: Frankie Valli, Bob Gaudio, Tommy DeVito, and Nick Massi. Each member of the Seasons narrates a fourth of the show, offering their own version of the events that led this band to fifteen Top Ten hits and a place in the Rock and Roll Hall of Fame. As they step on stage, the four actors playing the Seasons transform into rock stars. They sing, dance, play instruments, and live through two-and-a-half hours of the true-life events (mafia connections, robberies, gambling debts, drug overdoses, etc.) that brought the band together and, eventually, tore them apart.

That night in March, I was blown away by the show, and by the ensemble of actors and musicians backing the performers playing the Four Seasons. One of them, it turned out, is friend of mine. Colin is younger than me, a fresh face in New York, and an amazing performer. Reading the playbill, I realized that he was fairly new in the show and doing a smash-up job playing Hank Majewski, a member of the ensemble.

At the end of this performance I jumped to my feet with everyone else. I knew that there was a role in it for me. I just had a deep-inside-my-gut feeling that one day I would play Hank Majewski…

ACT I

TWO YEARS OF AUDITIONS

HANK MAJEWSKI, ELVIS TUNES, & VATS OF HAIR GEL

Every actor has their "audition protocol." Some actors will only go to auditions their agents have set up for them, while others will line up early to attend any audition at all, even if the audition is a required call. See, that's the thing about theatre auditions: shows are required to hold them even if they are not actually casting anything right then. This benefits the average actor, for it is often the only way they will be seen by the casting director of a given show.

Actors' Equity Association worked hard for this rule and I am grateful because I definitely fall into the latter category of auditioning. I will audition for anything. I have stood in line on 46th Street at 6:00 a.m. for days in a row during summer stock audition season. I have spent countless days in stairwells and hallways waiting three hours at a time to sign up for an audition, then two hours preparing for that audition later in the afternoon. It is routine to spend five hours in an audition room hoping for a slot while on the "alternate list" all because you spent the morning waiting for another audition ten blocks away.

And I am not alone. For these required auditions—the ones where the casting directors are not necessarily looking to actually cast the show—it is usual to have two hundred actors per day wanting to be seen. A moderate week may have eight of these auditions taking place. So that means there are sixteen hundred songs being sung for jobs that may not even exist.

There are two types of these required calls: Equity Principal Auditions (EPAs), which audition for principal roles, and chorus calls, which audition for ensemble roles. Chorus calls will typically allow an actor enough time for a mere sixteen bars of music. (Every actor knows sixteen bars of a hundred songs, but probably only knows the second verse to a handful.)

It's December, 2007. There is a required chorus call for *Jersey Boys* happening, and I know this is the perfect time to be seen for the role of Hank

Majewski. There seem to be productions of the show sprouting up everywhere, leaving quite a few guitar-playing actor slots to be filled.

The chorus call has two unique properties that play into my *Jersey Boys* beginnings. First, in addition to someone from the casting office attending, a musical director from the show is required to be present at all chorus calls. This doubles the chance of having someone actually pick you out of the crowd, and doubles the legitimacy of the experience. Second, chorus call slots may be claimed one week prior to the audition. This can guarantee that you will not have to wait around all day to sing, and helps me greatly because I teach workshops for a theatre company and have to find time to work these in. One week before the audition, I have one of these workshops I need to teach (gotta pay the bills), so I send Cara to the 2nd floor of the Actors' Equity building to sign me up.

Cara is the most creative and supportive fiancé a guy could ask for. Having both been married before, neither of us was looking for the relationship that eventually just kind of snuck up on us. We met at a theatre out west, and then worked through a long-distance relationship for about a year. One day during that year I realized that not only was I in love, but I had come to absolutely rely on her calming voice and unending belief in me. So we moved in together. We each came to the relationship with emotional baggage (who doesn't come to a relationship with emotional baggage?), but I am lucky to have found someone willing to work on "us" with fervor and commitment. She's my best friend.

I suppose I can locate my adoration for her in the events of our life together: She once drove ten hours to see me for my birthday when her flight was cancelled. She made me sleep outside at the edge of the Grand Canyon after a midnight arrival so that I would see it for the first time when the sun woke me at dawn. She cried in the moving van on the day we moved to New York City, not because of the lifestyle change, but because she saw a particularly destitute homeless man on the street. She told me very seriously how much she admired the effort I put in to an earlier book that never found its way to publication, and in doing so inspired my efforts on this one. And she even tells me that I am hotter than her celebrity crush, Duane "The Rock" Johnson.

It's funny that, given the opportunity to put in print exactly how I feel about Cara, I find her hard to describe. She is beautiful, surely—medium height, blond hair, great figure. But I suppose more specifics would be needed to pick her out of a lineup. (Thus far, no one has had to pick her out of a lineup.) Her hair is probably her most prominent feature—countless shades of blond and very thick, becoming even thicker as six or seven products are applied each day. Her blue eyes often seem to change color with her outfits, coordinating to their environment like a Bob Ross sky. She has long, thin, perfect eyebrows; made more perfect every three weeks by the Korean lady on 32nd Street. She also has a wide jaw that she doesn't care for, but I find to be strong and confident. And her collarbone is pronounced and sophisticated like a 1920's flapper.

I have never taken advantage of Cara's willingness to help me get an audition before this. (Sure she runs lines with me; but I must be frank and say that running lines is not quite in her skill set. She likes to read every word on the script's page, whether or not it is a line of dialogue. She reads aloud things like "Pause" and "Entering the Living Room" and "Juliet Picks Up the Dagger.") Cara works very late nights at *Saturday Night Live* in the hair department and waking early to sign me up for auditions is not part of our arrangement. So she makes me promise I will be cast in the show if I am going to make her get out of bed that early. So I promise.

This is a picture of Cara shortly after we met. It's my favorite picture of her, and reminds me of the first summer we spent together.

©Daniel Robert Sullivan

5

*   *   *

A week later, I arrive at the chorus call wearing a nice gray suit, black shirt, and gray tie, only to find I am one of a hundred with the same idea. While waiting to be called to sing, the casting director, Merri Sugarman, comes out to the waiting room and says hello to an actor I have seen around for years. Buck Hujabre looks like he belongs in the show. Innocent looking. Confident looking. Italian looking. He's perfect. And there is nothing more intimidating than discovering an actor you are competing with already has a relationship with the casting director. Oh, except discovering that there are a hundred guys in the room dressed the same as you. Oh, and also discovering that those same guys can sing the pants off you.

Cara has gotten me a decent audition number and I am in the room rather quickly. Ron Melrose, the musical director for *Jersey Boys* and creator of all the amazing new vocal arrangements of the songs, is in the room. I am not sure this is good news yet, as I have never been the best singer, and today (as proven by the sounds through the walls) I am nearer the bottom of the pack. But I have confidence in my ability to act. I can act the song better than anyone here! So I approach the piano with my music only to hear Ron say, "Just one thing I'm telling everybody, this show is not about acting the songs. It's just about the sound."

Ok. I guess I won't be playing Hank Majewski anytime soon. But I'm here, so I dive into sixteen bars of "Hurt," a song covered by Elvis Presley. I sang this song in an Elvis revue some years back, and it has a slow, steady beat that reminds me of early Four Seasons. When I am finished, Merri has on a polite smile and Ron says, "Thank you." I pick up my book of music, knowing "thank you" is an actor's cue to leave. As I am about to exit the room, a miracle occurs. Ron says, "Oh, hey. You play guitar. How well do you play?"

"I play pretty well," I say, and instantly thank my grandfather for giving my mother a Gibson when she was a teenager, a guitar that sat in our basement when I was a child so that one day I was bound to pick it up and ask for lessons.

*   *   *

Three days later I get a call from my agent. Meg Pantera is just about the best agent I could ask for. Her job is to get me auditions and negotiate contracts for me when I book work. Most people probably know that agents don't get paid unless the actor does. Now, I've been working lots of theatre jobs for many years, but I've been working mostly for small regional theatres and getting paid $250–$550 per week. When I send my agent her 10% commission check, it is embarrassingly small. When she negotiates a contract…well…there just isn't room to negotiate a thing. And yet she believes in me. Meg calls and says, "Dan, they want to see you for *Jersey Boys*." Well, Meg, I want to be seen for *Jersey Boys*. Oh boy, do I want to be seen for *Jersey Boys*.

As it turns out, Meg submitted my picture and resume to the casting director to be considered for an audition right about the same time I went to the chorus call of my own accord. This double-whammy scores me a coveted first audition. (Yes, first audition. They won't refer to it as a "callback," even though they already saw me at the chorus call.) I am to sing a 50s song, bring my guitar, and prepare some scenes that I will be emailed later today. The audition happens in a few days. I am ready to rock.

I get home and begin preparing some music. I have "Hurt," the song I have already shown them. And now I figure I should grab my electric guitar and learn something impressive and appropriate for the time period. I don't have a portable amplifier, so I buy a small battery-powered one and spend the day fooling around with various songs, finally landing on "Oh, What A Night." I realize that the song is performed in the show (which sometimes makes it a less cool choice), and that it was written in the 70s instead of the 50s. But I figure people know it as a piano song, whereas I will be rocking it hard on the electric guitar, which is pretty slick. And I do it well. It will be different, but not too different.

The scenes arrive in my inbox. They are a packet. The packet has a title: Bob. As in, *Bob Gaudio*. As in, one of the *lead roles*. What?! I call my agent. "I thought I was being considered for an ensemble role, like Hank Majewski. But Bob?! Is this for real?"

"Yes and no," she says. "I think they are looking for somebody to understudy Bob on the tour." Perfect. I've got this. Back to the scene packet…

It is twenty-seven pages long. And I have two days to learn it all.

*   *   *

The audition starts early, so I wake early. I take a long shower, drink a lot of coffee, grease up my hair, put on a suit, review my lines, tune my guitar, and rehearse my songs. I walk to the audition studio (conveniently close to our apartment), re-tune the guitar, use the bathroom, check on my slicked-back hair, sing a bit in the stairwell, and review my lines again. This is already becoming a routine; a long routine! A routine that I hope to repeat a few times if they like my audition today.

My name is called. I go into a small audition studio I have been in many times before, so I feel comfortable there. It has hardwood floors, a giant mirror, and windows looking into an alleyway. The only people present are Casting Director Merri Sugarman, the accompanist, and a reader. Merri asks if I would prefer to sing with the piano or accompany myself on the guitar. I have worked up this killer version of my song, so I opt for the guitar straightaway. I set up the miniature amp and launch into my rockin' version of "Oh, What A Night" with giant power chords on the electric guitar.

I finish.

It is quiet.

"Dan."

"Yes?"

"Didn't your agent tell you not to sing a song from the show?"

No, she didn't tell me not to sing a song from the show! And she is very good and very organized, so I bet someone just forgot to tell her to tell me not to sing a song from the show! And I just sang a song from the show!

"Dan."

"Yes?"

"If we bring you back again, we'd also prefer you bring an acoustic guitar instead of an electric."

Please note that there are no acoustic guitars in *Jersey Boys*. But I'm not going to bring that up right this minute.

She asks me to sing another song, so I dive into the first one that comes to mind, a rockabilly tune recorded by Elvis Presley: "That's All Right, Mama." This is now the second Elvis song I have sung for Merri. You'd think I was in Las Vegas or something. I finish my audition by performing just a few pages of the twenty-seven I have memorized. The reader assigned to do the scenes with me also has them memorized, so I get the impression he has done this many, many times today. And yesterday. And last month.

I'm done and I go home.

*   *   *

Wonder of wonders! Miracle of miracles! I get a callback. I'm told to come back next week with the same twenty-seven pages of script. I am being considered for the ensemble role of Norm, a role that understudies Bob but also has quite a few juicy scenes himself. I am beside myself. I vow never to touch the electric guitar again, and I work up a better version of "That's All Right, Mama" on an acoustic. Instead of doing the song as it was written, I add a key change so that they can see I really know how to play the guitar. I don't know how to finish the song though, so I play it for Cara and stop abruptly after the second verse. She takes over the singing, putting in a groovy little ritard and high note on the last line. It sounds perfect; I figure out how to play it and now have a tight little selection of music.

The callback takes place in the same location as the last audition, Chelsea Studios in Manhattan. I wake early, take a long shower, drink a gallon of coffee, grease up my hair, put on a suit, review my lines, tune my guitar, and rehearse my songs. I walk to the audition studio, re-tune the guitar, use the bathroom, check on my slicked-back hair, sing a bit in the stairwell, and review my lines again. Is this sounding familiar yet?

Buck, the actor who looked perfect at the chorus call, is at this callback. I introduce myself and we talk. We are both excited. He is a kindred spirit.

They call my name and Merri gives me a very cheerful welcome. I've come to understand that Merri is terrifically direct and efficient at her job. She clearly loves what she does and adores working with actors, but she is also very much a straight shooter and won't hesitate to make your life clearer by telling you when you've done something wrong. (Or right! But mostly wrong.)

I enter the room and see the very same people who were there the last time. This callback feels exactly the same as the first audition, so I can only

9

imagine that there are just fewer actors being seen today; Merri must be holding this callback just to keep her own head straight.

The Elvis song goes well. The scenes feel pretty good. Merri gives me some direction about how to play Bob, and I try one of the scenes again. She seems pleased enough and calls me over to the table while she writes something on a scrap of paper. It is an address. She says, "We'd like to see you dance on Friday at this location."

Wonder of wonders! Miracle of mira... wait. Dance? I think I just heard the word, *dance*. Nothing scares me more than the word *dance*. There are very few times in my life when I have been seen dancing, and every one of them was because I was flirting with a certain girl at a certain bar out west. I am engaged to that girl now. And Cara can't get me to dance anymore.

But dancing is what I have to do, and I have to do it in two days.

I walk home, trying to think of what I can do to give myself some sort of leg up with this dancing. I am considering taking a dance class, just to get my body moving in some kind of rhythm, when I am smacked with the perfect idea. There are lots of YouTube videos of *Jersey Boys*, right? And there is bound to be choreography from the actual show at this dance audition, right? So I am going to learn every bit of choreography I can before Friday!

Now I rush home. I push the rug back in our bedroom, put the computer up against our mirror, and find the four best *Jersey Boys* videos available online. Cara comes home, happy that I am being called back again and hysterical at the idea of me learning choreography in our small bedroom. So what does she do? She vows to learn it with me. And for the next forty-eight hours we are dancing "Who Loves You" and "Walk Like A Man" in our socks, crammed between our king-size bed and two bureaus. Funny girl, that soon-to-be wife of mine.

In addition to being my bedroom dance partner, Cara is also a mother who brought two surprises to my life: her children, Mark and Rachel. Mark is a creative and laid-back teenager attending Art And Design High School in Manhattan with the ability to do just about anything he sets his mind to, and Rachel is just about the most perfect little girl in the world, made even more perfect in my eyes by her recent love for musical theatre. (She learned

Shakira songs long ago, but now she knows every word to *The Phantom of the Opera*.) Together, we are a very blond, blended family unit. And for two nights, Mark seems just a bit embarrassed that our window shades remain open while Cara and I learn choreography in our room.

The dance call takes place in the rehearsal studio of the Hilton Theatre (soon to be known as the Foxwoods Theatre, home to the infamous *Spiderman: Turn Off the Dark*). The Hilton is one of the biggest theatres on Broadway, and its rehearsal studio is even bigger. I show up with some semblance of dance attire. You see, real dancers always wear funky, tight, cool-looking dance clothes. And guys who don't dance at all (and want everyone to know it) wear sweat pants and a loose t-shirt. I am not a real dancer, but I certainly don't want to project that I am a bad one! So I put together a dance outfit that is not funky like a real dancer might wear, but that is form fitting, black, and cool enough.

There are many guys at this audition. Maybe twenty-five of them. I didn't expect anything less, but I admit I was hoping there would be an elite group of five or six. But there are twenty-five, and it is just as I expected: some are clearly dancers and ready to impress, and some are guys who belong in a football locker room wearing old sweat pants and baggy Hard Rock Cafe t-shirts.

Many people are warming up by stretching and moving, others are demonstrating that they are not dancers by half mocking the stretching. This is a common occurrence, one I have come to understand as a confidence-boosting technique. When you are in a room with a lot of people who you already know are going to be better dancers than you, it helps your ego to sort of mock the process and set yourself apart as someone different. The show you put on says, "I am here because I am a great actor, or a great singer, and this dancing bit is just a requirement, a mandatory (but unimportant) step in the process of them giving me a part..." It is a show that I have put on myself, though I think I've grown out of it. I hope I've grown out of it. Ok, I probably haven't grown out of it. But on this day, I do not participate.

This is a very recent picture of Mark and Rachel, both of them looking very, very old!

*   *   *

Peter Gregus walks into the room. Peter Gregus originated the role of Bob Crewe in the Broadway cast of *Jersey Boys* and remains in the show to this day. He is also the dance captain and will teach us the choreography. "Good morning, guys! Stretch your right legs 'cuz we'll be doing the splits." Um. Ok. The splits. I don't remember there being any splits in *Jersey Boys*.

We begin with a hip-hop routine. This is the choreography that opens the show. It was not available to watch on YouTube, so I'm fearing the worst. He teaches us the choreography fast and, much to my surprise, I feel ok with it.

While I am certainly not great, I actually remember it all when we run it together as a group. Then Peter says, "Ok, we're going to add a finish to this bit. I want you all to throw your right arm in the air and do the splits." He is serious. He demonstrates. I try. I fail…big time. In fact, I cannot even fathom how some of the guys can make their legs do that.

We move on to a second routine, which turns out to be exactly what I've been working on with Cara in our apartment. Now we're in business! They play "Who Loves You" on the piano, and I feel one step ahead of Peter as he teaches us the moves. Now, I may not do them well (I'm still no dancer), but remembering the steps is 90% of the battle for me, and I am confident I will remember them all.

And I get lucky. There is one swaying and snapping move that Cara constantly poked fun at me about. I just couldn't get it to look right. I could do the whole routine, but would have to stop at this place because my body just can't move the way those boys' did on YouTube. But this swaying move has been left out of the combination today! I don't have to do it; and that means I am even more confident that I will rock this section. After a quick group review, the real audition begins.

Merri Sugarman comes into the room and introduces us to Sergio Trujillo. Sergio is the choreographer of *Jersey Boys*, an unbelievable dancer in his own right, and a big-time star in the theatre world. He is amazing to watch, has a reputation for being extremely specific with what he wants from actors auditioning for him, and is very intimidating to have in the room. Quickly, he and Merri take seats in the front of the room and all of us actors are asked to stand to the side. He calls out a group of three to the center of the floor, and right away music begins for the hip-hop routine. Three guys do the splits. Two guys do it beautifully, and the third guy probably won't walk straight for a year.

The dancers are given only a few seconds to breathe before music begins for the second routine. They launch into it, do pretty well (except that poor guy who seems very much affected by his splits), and are sent back to the side of the room.

Three more guys are called. While they dance, I run through the routine in my head at the side of the room. Unfortunately, it is not socially acceptable to actually do the dance at the side of the room. Honestly, I am not sure why this is the case, but I know that you will be asked to stop if you try it. Probably has to do with keeping the choreographer's focus clear on what is happening in the center. But I run through it in my head so I do not forget a step.

It's my turn. About half the guys have danced so far. They place me at the center of the three of us, meaning I will finish my splits right in front of Sergio. We do the hip-hop routine and I remember every step. I feel cool. I act manly. I sweat so much that my fingertips drip. That's right, my fingertips. I do the splits and, though I don't even come close to getting them to the floor, I do the move cleanly and simply—and I don't fall over. I stand up with a bit of a confident smile and get ready for the next routine. Which I rock! Oh, thank God for those lessons in my bedroom. I am sent back to the side of the room to wait with the others.

When all the guys have danced, Merri and Sergio take a few minutes to shuffle through our headshots. Then, the moment of truth. Merri says, "Thank you all for coming out here this morning. Special thank you to the two guys who flew in from Chicago for this. We are going to keep nine of you for a bit longer, but the rest of you are free to go home." Being free to go home means you are no longer being considered for this show. Oh, I'm sure you could audition again in the future and improve your situation, but really it means that the two months you've just spent in callbacks have been ruined by the reaction to your dancing. I am not looking forward to being "free to go home."

"Will the following people please stick around? David Richardson. Franklin Miller. Joseph Killian."

PAUSE

"Brian Krantz."

LONGER PAUSE

"Michael Lambert."

REALLY LONG, COMPLETELY NERVE-WRACKING PAUSE

14

"Brett Lahey. Daniel Robert Sullivan." I get to stay! Two more names are called, but I certainly cannot hear them with all the cheering going on inside my head. We nine are asked to come again to the center of the room in groups of three and perform both dance combinations. With no direction given, it seems Sergio just wants to get a better handle on what we can do. I do the routines pretty much the same as before, although I have much less nervous energy now. I feel a bit surer of myself now that I know I have been kept. Buck is also kept. He must have been one of the last two names called. That guy just keeps following me.

When we are all finished showing our stuff a second time, Sergio thanks us and asks us all to speak to Merri privately in the hallway. But first he'd like to see three guys privately himself: a guy named Howie Michael Smith, a guy with curly hair, and me. Now I really have no idea whether this is a good thing or a bad thing. It could very easily be, "These guys are my favorites," or "Merri says these guys are well-liked, but they didn't do well enough for me, so I guess I have to work them a bit more and see if they can cut it." Sergio gives us no clue as to why he has kept us, but I look at the situation favorably because of the company I keep. I have never seen the curly-haired guy before, but Howie is currently playing the lead role in *Avenue Q* on Broadway. He is well-respected, well-liked, and very talented—so I am leaning towards this work session being a good thing.

We are taught just one move: a snapping step-touch that three of the actors do for their first entrance. It looks like a simple step, but Sergio is extremely precise (his reputation holds true). My back must be at this angle, my arms at that angle, my foot a little more behind the beat...ugh! It is not difficult to do the move, but very difficult to be so precise. When we finish this private session, he thanks us (oh no, Sergio, thank you!) and sends us out for our private talk with Merri. The guy with the curly hair did really well, so I expect him to be happy when he is called over to speak with Merri first. But she has a look on her face that projects some sympathy and he, a bit too loudly perhaps, says, "Awww, come on." And he leaves. Angrily.

My turn. And I hear the magic words, "We'd like you to come back later." Woo-hoo! Thank God for YouTube!

I leave the building, and Howie stays in *Avenue Q* for another two years.

With nothing really to do and an hour before it seems all right to go back in the building, I wander the streets of Midtown and dream. Seriously, I have never been

15

this close to something this big in my life. People like to say it is pointless to get your hopes up, but if I didn't get my hopes up I would be depressed all the time. Each audition creates a possibility of my childhood dream coming true, so I love these moments when the hard work is done and I can dream a bit about what might happen.

When I can't wander anymore, and feel the audition rooms are empty enough that it would be all right to take over the bathroom there, I go back and change into my suit and tie. I comb my hair into a nice parted style and tune up my guitar. I review all the scenes, although by now I have them solidly memorized. I polish my shoes. I transform into a Bob understudy.

Five guys participate in this round, Buck included. While he was not one of the three kept for additional dancing with Sergio, he has been brought back for this session, proving that...well actually it proves nothing. It only reinforces the idea that an actor can never really know what the people on the other side of the table are thinking. I was asked to dance some more; Buck wasn't. I was asked to come back later; Buck was too. (Auditioning this way reminds me of doing my taxes—I never really know what the result is going to be until it's over. There are so many little variations and calculations that an amount owed could come just as easily as a refund.)

I hear Buck through the walls. He's good. When it's my turn, I enter the room and am introduced to Richard Hester, the production supervisor, and Ron Melrose, the musical director who may or may not remember me. These guys are well known and again I am very intimidated. But at least now I know that I have done a solid enough job to get this far, and I am very confident about how they want me to play these scenes. I do my Elvis song, perform a few of the scenes, and they seem pleased. They tell me they would like to bring me in to meet Des McAnuff. Des is the two-time Tony Award-winning director of *Jersey Boys*. He is totally famous. He is totally cool. He is totally in charge. And I am totally scared. (But excited! But scared.) On my way out, Ron asks me if I have ever tried playing the drums.

"Not really," I say, "but I have pretty good rhythm." (This is a totally dumb thing to say.) He advises me that some of the ensemble roles that understudy Bob have to play the drums, and suggests that maybe I should "take a lesson sometime."

The next day I start drum lessons. Through Cara's connections, I am able to get in touch with a drummer who actually played on the *Jersey Boys* cast recording.

How'd this happen? Cara walked into the orchestra pit at a Broadway show she was subbing in on last night (she fills in at various hair departments for side work when she can) and asked all the musicians for suggestions on who to call for instruction.

I meet this drummer at his studio a few times. He doesn't usually give lessons but is making an exception for me. Now, I am a guy who taps his fingers on everything. If I had drums on my thighs, I would be a masterful player. But let me tell you something: playing real drums with real drumsticks is not at all like playing thigh-drums with your fingertips. Playing real drums is hard. I learn all these introductory exercises, but let's be real here: where am I going to practice? If I rent a drum room, I am just skyrocketing the cost of learning. If I try to drum on a pillow or a practice board, it just doesn't feel the same. Rhythm is not my problem. I play guitar—a rhythmic instrument. The actual hitting of the drum with the stick while using my left foot to move the cymbal and my right foot to work the bass drum causes a problem. It is hard, seemingly impossible work! And I just want to go meet Des.

So I do. The following week I am asked to come down to Chelsea Studios, where my first auditions took place, and be seen by Des. As the routine goes: I wake early, take a long shower, drink coffee, grease up my hair, put on a suit, review my lines, tune my guitar, and rehearse my songs. I walk to the studio, re-tune the guitar, use the bathroom, check my hair, sing in the stairwell, and review my lines again. Buck is here. He has been through every step of this process with me and is up for the exact same role. So I punch him and drag him into the stairwell. (No, I don't!)

They call me into the audition room, which is pretty full. The usual people I've seen at the previous auditions are all here, plus an additional crop of producers, assistants, and interns. And Des. Oh, Des. I bring my guitar to the side of the room and say hello to everyone. Des looks at me, then turns toward Merri and begins to whisper. I pull out my guitar and am ready to begin, but he continues to whisper and, now, he points at me! Finally he says, "Ok, I'm having a bit of a problem here, but why don't you sing something anyway?" Perfect.

I sing my Elvis song, and Des asks me about my guitar. I play an Ovation, which has a rounded back. It's a lightweight, versatile guitar that is great for fast, rocking tunes. And Des likes it. He used to play one in his band, he says. (He is so

17

cool.) He has me do just one of the scenes, then calls me closer. "I like you," he says. "I have an issue that I'm going to have them talk to your agent about, but I want you to know that I like you and we're going to send you to see the show."

What does all this mean?!

Not until the next morning do I find out. It turns out that when I walked in the room, Des instantly decided I am not going to be a Bob, a Bob understudy, a Bob swing, or anything whatsoever having to do with Bob. I do not look like a Bob, he says, I look like a Tommy. Tommy DeVito. The bad boy. The bad-ass. The role that won Christian Hoff his Tony Award. Me. A Tommy.

Tommy DeVito was born in the tough neighborhoods outside of Newark, New Jersey and is as first-generation Italian as they come. I was born in the sailboat-laden beaches of Newport, Rhode Island and am as fifth-generation Irish as they come. While Tommy robbed a jewelry store to get some spending cash for horse races and weekends in Atlantic City, I dressed up as a giant pint of Ben & Jerry's ice cream to pay for magic tricks from Winkler's Warehouse of Wonders. This contradiction doesn't seem to bother anybody.

I am to stop by the casting director's office to pick up a dialect CD and a new scene packet. I will also be sent to see *Jersey Boys* on Broadway for free so that I can watch with an eye towards this new character.

And by the way, they did make a decision as to who will be the new Bob understudy. Buck got the job.

*　　　　　*　　　　　*

When I arrive at the casting office, it turns out to be much smaller than I expected. I mean, this is Tara Rubin Casting. They cast all companies of *Phantom of the Opera, Mamma Mia, Billy Elliot, Spamalot, Young Frankenstein*, and about a bajillion others. The walls of the only room are lined with files, presumably files full of actor headshots and resumes. This is insane to see. There are hundreds and hundreds of these files, and they are (obviously) just the ones they felt were good enough to save. Imagine how many were thrown out! Which reminds me…

Some years ago, on the Upper West Side, there was a trash bag full of headshots and resumes that some casting director had thrown out. The bag had split open and was spilling onto the sidewalk. An astute pedestrian called the *New York Post* and they promptly published a picture of this "pile of broken dreams." (And they didn't overlook the fact that there were hundreds of photos of beautiful girls in this pile with phone numbers in big typeface at the top of their resumes.) The casting director apologized; but really, that is the reality. When hundreds of people audition, hundreds of pictures will be thrown in the trash. Someone with a healthy conscience, like my agent, brings rejected headshots away from the city before disposing of them. That way it lessens the chance of the pictures being exposed or examined.

But I digress... Tara Rubin's casting office is fun to look at, and Merri welcomes me in. She gives me the dialect CD. She gives me new material to learn for the role of Tommy. Thirty-three pages. Yup, thirty-three. And she gives me instructions on who to talk to at the August Wilson Theatre to see the show as their guest.

"So, Des really liked you yesterday," Merri tells me.

"Well, I'm sure glad about that," I say in my best professional voice, "but I was surprised about him liking me for Tommy."

"Not as surprised as we were," she says. Do I detect a note of exasperation in her voice? "But Des is always right."

I am sure not going to debate that. On my way out, one of the assistants goes out of her way to tell me that she saw my audition and thought it was great. I'm not going to lie, that is really encouraging to hear.

The next day, I hire a vocal coach to teach me Tommy's songs. The audition material sounds similar to what you hear in the show, but it's not exactly the same. I don't play piano, so I am forever hiring people to help me learn music. I often think of how much easier life would be if I took some basic piano lessons or learned how to teach myself music. But then I think of the time it would take to practice and I become unwilling. Were I to practice piano, I would have far less time to go to the theatre, read *Scientific American*, call my mom, eat nachos late at night with Cara, and research money-making schemes like gambling systems and book publishing. Some people spend money on cabs because they don't want to invest the time it takes to walk; I spend money on vocal coaches for a similar reason.

Daniel Robert Sullivan

My coach is great, supportive, and also surprised that I am being considered for this particular bad-ass role. She knows that I have had success playing the sweet and innocent Finch in *How to Succeed in Business Without Really Trying*. She also knows that my first regional theatre job was playing the sweet and innocent Rolf in *The Sound of Music*, and that my latest was playing Leo Davis in *Room Service*, who is (you guessed it) sweet and innocent. Tommy DeVito, in real life, grew up the youngest of nine kids in the poorest part of Belleville, New Jersey. He stole his first car at fourteen. He was arrested for the first time at fifteen. He worked for a mob boss in his early days, and in his later days was accused of money laundering in connection with an attempted bribe of Richard Nixon. This role is a bit of a stretch for me.

*   *   *

Three days later I am entering through the stage door of the August Wilson Theatre. Upon arriving, I tell the security guard I am to check in with the stage management office. What I really want to tell him is that I have been auditioning for this show for a couple months now and it feels like they might be interested in me and this is the first time I have ever been this close to a big job in a blockbuster musical and I have dreamed about this since I was in fifth grade playing "Colonel Cuddly" in a Christmas pageant and I have been sent to see the show today because Des, that's right, Des McAnuff, thinks that I might be a Tommy and I am ready with a pen to take notes on what I see and I am so nervous and excited that I've used the bathroom three times in the past hour…but I just say, "Which way do I go?"

I check in with stage management. They give me a sticker that says "CAST." Oh yes. They lead me through a vast array of underground twists and turns (these old Broadway theatres are cramped and have lots of underground spaces) which eventually brings us out into the lobby. They introduce me to the house manager and she tells me to stand in the back of the house until about fifteen minutes into the show when she will come get me and move me to an empty seat, if one is available.

The show begins, and I am hooked once again. I feel a bubbling in my stomach. It's a good kind of bubbling, not an awkward kind. When Christian

Hoff makes his entrance as Tommy I am no longer watching with joy and excitement, but rather with focused attention. I take notes in my program. (I didn't want to bring a notebook for fear of looking dumb, but in retrospect it is much dumber taking notes in a program that doesn't have any blank pages.) I write down anything that Christian does that is not an "obvious" interpretation, and that is a lot. There is a good reason he won the Tony for this role. He exudes nuance and lovable bad-boy qualities. I envy him. I want to emulate him.

When the show is over, I am filled with a wonderful sense of privilege. I feel lucky to be able to work on this role, lucky to be here watching the show as their guest, and extremely lucky to be respected by the creative team. Whether or not I will ever get the role does not even cross my mind this night. (Well, almost.) Overwhelmed with the possibility, I come out of the show believing I could do this part.

*   *   *

Months go by. That's right, months. I do not report back to the casting director's office with my thoughts on the show, nor do they call to see how I'm doing with the Jersey accent. The theatre world doesn't work that way. The theatre world is one of waiting. One in which the actor must be remarkably independent in preparing for possible work, and remarkably patient while waiting for any actual work to appear.

I do a play. I teach. I have my regular New York life. Finally, I get a call from my agent. They would like to bring me in to audition again, this time for Tommy. Bear in mind that there is no actual job available. The casting people have such a long hiring process that they really just need to keep updating their files with people who are approved or working their way towards being approved. But the reality is that there are only five companies of *Jersey Boys* currently in North America, and that means there are only five Tommy jobs available. I am very lucky to have gotten this far, but it still doesn't mean that one of the five guys playing this role is going to leave. Ever.

And I keep track of those possibilities too! Since much time has gone by, I have become obsessed with checking the *Jersey Boys* Fan Forum. There are hundreds of die-hard fans who share, chat, and gossip about the show online. Believe it or not, the collective fact-gathering of the folks on this site has kept me in the loop about the comings and goings of each company. I know that the San Francisco Tommy became the Tour Tommy and was replaced by a guy who would become the Chicago Tommy until he left to be the Vegas Tommy and they got a new Chicago Tommy, and then the original Tour Tommy became the Vegas Tommy while the Vegas Tommy became the Tour Tommy until he opened as the Toronto Tommy and the Tour Tommy (who was a temporary Vegas Tommy) went on the road, to be replaced by his understudy as the Tour Tommy when he went to be the understudy for the new Broadway Tommy, who was formerly the understudy for the original Broadway Tommy. Thank you, Al Gore, for creating the internet.

Armed with a head full of cast-change gossip, I know that my audition today probably isn't for any current job opening. But I prepare my billion-page scene packet, two songs from the score ("Earth Angel" and "Silhouettes"), and my trusty Elvis tune. And I review all the notes I took while watching Christian Hoff. I wake early for the audition and repeat my routine: coffee, long shower, reviewing, walking to studio, re-tuning, reviewing…and I am called in. Merri is there with just an assistant and a reader. She tells me that she only wanted to bring me in because I have not done the Tommy material for her yet. Does she want me to sing? No. Play guitar? No. She just wants me to do the scenes.

So I do them. I pretty much just copy Christian Hoff as much as I can. This seems to suffice (for now) and she gives me some positive feedback. The last scene she asks me to do is the one where Tommy hits on a reporter at a bar. Because the reader is male, Merri says that she will do the scene with me. She's a good actress, but boy is this awkward for me! I have, through this entire audition process, presented myself as "the nice guy." Playing Tommy, though, I have to show more attitude, cockiness, and balls. And nowhere do I have to show it more than in this scene I am doing with a famous casting director, the same casting director who holds my future in her hands.

I dive in, and the scene goes well. I diffuse my own awkwardness at the end of it with a little laugh and an acknowledgment that it was a bit weird for me. Merri chuckles as well, but she is probably just being polite. She's done this many times with many other actors and must be very used to it by now.

*　　　　　　　*　　　　　　　*

23

Another month passes. Regular life resumes. Well, regular life with a heavy dose of checking the *Jersey Boys* Fan Forum every morning. There is absolutely no hint of cast changes. In fact, I am getting the impression that *Jersey Boys* really just shifts people around instead hiring someone new. They are loyal to this core group of actors they have hired. Whether for financial or ethical reasons I do not know, but it is neat to see. I just have to get into that core group of actors!

I get a call from my agent, "Dan, they want to call you back for the role of Tommy."

"Meg, can you still refer to it as a callback after all this time?" I ask her, but I think my joke gets lost in her sea of phone calls, voicemails, emails, and contracts being negotiated for folks much more successful than I.

So, off I go to refresh myself on the material. (Ok, I don't really need to refresh myself on the material because I have been carrying it around in my backpack every day for the past year. Sure, one day I switched it from the Bob material to the Tommy material, but that manila envelope filled with scenes and music has not left my side since last year.)

The morning of the audition, I wake, drink forty-three gallons of coffee, take a thirty-six hour shower, review the material, put three vats of gel in my hair, and am ready to head on my way when my soon-to-be stepson, Mark, stops me. This is my first *Jersey Boys* audition taking place on a Saturday and, therefore, the first time Mark has seen me greased up and in my dark suit (and with attitude).

"Daniel, you look tough." Mark, that is about the greatest possible thing you could have said to me. "Where are you going?"

"*Jersey Boys* audition."

"Again?"

"Yup. Again."

"For Broadway or somewhere else?"

"Well, I don't know. They don't tell me that."

"When would it start?"

"Well, they don't tell me that either. Actually, I don't even know if there is a part available."

"If there is no part available, why are you auditioning?"

"That's just how they do it."

24

"They have auditions when there are no parts?"

"Yup. All the time."

"And you keep getting asked to come back to these auditions over and over?"

"Yup."

"Even though there are no parts?"

"Yup."

"Over and over?"

"Yup."

"I don't get it."

"Neither do I." And we both stand there with Godot-like stillness.

The callback, with all the same Tommy material, is with Merri and Richard Hester, the production supervisor. He knows this show inside and out, and tells me precisely what Des McAnuff wants to see. I am still pretty much doing an impersonation of Christian Hoff, but Richard shakes me of that when he gives me notes that are different from what Christian does. I think Richard is trying to shape a Tommy that lives truthfully in me, and I guess I should start doing the same.

The audition ends with them telling me that they will be bring me in to see Des again the next time he is in town. This, too, seems to be part of the *Jersey Boys* thing. In order to be hired, you need approval from Des, but Des only comes in to town once in a while. So the casting team preps me (and many others) early so that when Des gets in to town we are ready to go.

*   *   *

And...another month. A lot more life goes by. I suppose everybody knows that actors often have day jobs. I am no exception. When I was in college at the University of Rhode Island, I knew that my chosen life was probably going to need a backup plan. So I had a triple major and received degrees not only in Acting (BFA), but in Secondary Education (BS) and English (BA). I later went on to receive my MFA in Acting and Directing at the University of Missouri/Kansas City with the thought that one day I may want to teach at a college; and one needs a Master's degree to do that legitimately, right? But

25

being a regular teacher while looking for acting work wasn't a possibility, for it made attending any auditions impossible. So when I moved to New York for the first time in 1998, I tried a number of day jobs; jobs that were flexible, so I could wait in line for an audition in the morning and attend it in the afternoon:

Substitute Teacher: I took my teaching certification down to the Board of Education, was fingerprinted, and received the paperwork required to be a sub. But in order to get work, I needed to visit specific principals and ask to be put on the school's roster. After visiting a number of these principals, and having most claim they had enough subs already, I received calls for work from only one. And the work was unreliable. As you probably realize, a sub gets a call early in the morning to come in that day. These calls were sporadic on days I had free and could not be accepted on days when I attended auditions.

Subway Musician: This remains the most lucrative hourly wage I've ever made. I started taking my guitar down into the subway to sing and play music for money. It was perfect in that I could set my own hours and work only as much as I wanted or needed to. I became aware that a certain structure exists in the underground music world. For example, I learned that people who play in the subway stations have to audition and register with the city if they want to play in certain key locations or if they want to play with amplification. I did not want to be terribly official, so I found a nice, unregulated, high-traffic area in the tunnel between 7th and 8th Avenues along 42nd Street, a tunnel that resonated enough that I didn't need amplification.

There was a reggae player there who usually stopped playing around 2:00 p.m., and I would try to take over after him each day. He was a big stoner, lived in Harlem, and loved to tell me about his many girlfriends. He also played the same song ("Redemption Song") for an hour or more, asserting, "It's the song that makes me the most money, bro." So I stole this technique; my guitar rendition of "Piano Man" (with a harmonica strapped around my neck) could be heard every day for way, way too long. After me, there was a clarinet player who paid rent on his West Village apartment by playing down in the tunnels, and was always trying to get me to hang out with him. Nice guy, but I didn't think it wise to mingle too much with the underground world.

I enjoyed this time of my life. I enjoyed having a hundred songs memorized and ready to play. And I loved how my guitar became splattered with blood because I would literally play until my fingers bled. I only stopped using this as my day job when I began to feel the effects of singing balls-out for four hours every day. It was fun, but it started to hurt.

Telephone Psychic: Yes, that's right. I was a psychic on a telephone hotline and it was a complete scam. I thought it'd be the perfect job when I applied. I could sit at home and make money while I watched TV! I could set my own hours, at any time I could call in and say that I was "on the clock." And then I would wait for the phone to ring. Did I have to be a real psychic? No. For the interview, I was asked to give a tarot reading over the phone to a company representative. Tarot cards are images, subject to the interpretation of their dealer, and so I gave a wonderfully positive reading to my boss, a reading that I made up off the top of my head. She said I was great and I was hired. But after a few days of listening to how many people actually believed in this stuff, and after seeing how few times my phone rang each hour (for employees are paid by the minute), I quit. Despite my quick tenure, I still tend to favor these stories more than any others when I'm at a party.

Gambler: By now, everyone must have heard of the MIT Blackjack Team. I too became obsessed with the idea of outsmarting a casino, albeit with far fewer credentials than those guys at MIT. With a gem of an idea from a Kansas City friend, I believed (don't make fun) that I could minimize the casino advantage in mini-Baccarat to its lowest possible point and keep wins at the highest possible dollar amount. I believed I would win 49% of the time with straight, structured play. I'm not a foolish guy. And I love math. And I know that gambling systems never work in the long run. Even though the casino still had an advantage in this game, I felt it was a small enough one to risk, so I spent a couple months turning a $2000 stake into $21,000 in my free time. I say again, I am not so dumb as to have believed it could have kept working, so I stopped just in time. It was a strong high to sit there in a smoky room and throw down chips while the pit boss doled out comps. I earned so many free blueberry muffins and cups of iced tea from the casino deli that I lost count.

New York City Tour Guide: I took a test to get my official tour guide license and began narrating tours of the city on those double-decker busses you see

27

everywhere. That was a neat adventure. Tours were given on an uptown or downtown route and a guide could talk about whatever seemed appropriate or interesting. We had to purchase our own microphones (for sanitary reasons, I guess) and were allowed to ask for tips. Asking for tips was, in fact, a necessary part of the job, for the wage we received was very, very low. I had some good jokes, I'd throw in lots of theatre trivia, and I generally liked being in control of the tourist's experience. I was an entertaining guide, but not an extremely knowledgeable one; I pointed out the Chrysler Building on my first nighttime tour and said, "Ladies and Gentlemen, if you look to your left you'll see the Empire State Building all lit up." I've learned since then.

Shakespeare Ticket Line-Sitter: Every summer in New York, the Public Theatre offers free tickets to their Shakespeare in the Park series. Seeing a performance of such high quality in a setting as beautiful as the Delacorte Theatre in Central Park is a quintessential New York experience. The catch to these free tickets is that you have to wait in line for about seven hours; and the wait begins around 6:00 a.m. An entrepreneurial business developed in which many people without anything else to do (i.e. actors between jobs) would wait in line for you, for a fee of $100–$150. I spent a few weeks of a summer doing just this, and am thankful that I did it before Attorney General Andrew Cuomo began publicly cracking down on the practice.

Knock-Off Purse Re-Seller: (I shouldn't be writing about this one.) I spent a period of time going down to Chinatown and buying knock-off Coach handbags from secret rooms and the back of vans. I'd talk them down to a rock-bottom price, then re-sell them online for a $20 profit on each one. I did not pretend they were real Coach products, for as good as they looked on the outside there was no way they could have been real for that price. I once bought a handbag with a statement stamped on the inside that read, "This is an authentic Coach scarf."

Teaching Artist: My greatest day job. A day job that has been so fulfilling, lucrative, flexible, and interesting that it has now turned into a side career. I have worked, on and off, since 2000 as a Master Teaching Artist with the Roundabout Theatre Company. Roundabout is one of the nation's largest non-profit theatre companies, operating three Broadway and two Off-Broadway theatres. My work there has varied, including teaching arts-integrated residencies at New York City

High Schools, leading professional development workshops for teachers, leading public speaking workshops for corporate managers, coordinating partnerships between Roundabout and certain partner schools, delivering dramaturgical lectures before the Roundabout's Broadway shows, and moderating post-show discussions at those same performances. What a gift to be able to balance the art (and health insurance) from my work in small regional theatres with the intellectual challenges (and salary) of this Roundabout job.

*   *   *

After months of waiting, I finally get a call saying Des will be in town and would like to see me perform the Tommy material. I am nearly certain that there are no actual jobs available at this point, but I go through the old routine of preparation anyway. I realize too late that I have run out of ordinary hair gel, and begin looking for something to give my hair the wet and dark look I have gone with all along. (I'm a pale, blond, Irish guy, so I need to do whatever I can to look more like the dark Italian they want.) I find only one product in our apartment that will do the job, but it frightens me a little—Murray's Pomade.

Those that have used Murray's Pomade know that it requires a month-long commitment. The stuff just won't wash out. You can scrub it, comb it, scour it, or hit it with an industrial-strength sand blaster and it still won't come out. I run a palm-full through my hair and ask Cara if she will cut some of it out later. She digs around for the electric carving knife just in case I'm serious.

I arrive at the studio and am the only Tommy there. This assures me that every performing Tommy in North America is very happy in his job and will not be leaving anytime soon. That's too bad for me, but at least it lessens my emotional burden. I am less nervous knowing this is just another step in the process. There are a few Bobs auditioning, and one of them resonates through the walls with such power that I glance over at another actor (auditioning for the part of Nick) and whisper, "Wow."

"Yeah. He's got it, huh?" the Nick says.

I agree, "Sounds that way to me." That resonating voice belongs to Quinn VanAntwerp, and it will land him the part.

29

When I am called into the room, I am greeted with warmth and, dare I say, affection by Merri, Des, and the rest of the team. Des makes it clear from the first moment that he just wants to see what I've been able to do with the material, and that he doesn't actually need a Tommy right now. No problem, Des. Ready to rock and roll. I play the scenes with subtle power and as much attitude as I can muster. Des says, and I will never forget these words, "I can see you've worked a lot on this." Um. Yes, Des. I have been carrying around these new pages everywhere I go, reviewing them on the subway and running them while I work out, while also studying Christian Hoff's gestures on YouTube and speaking in a Jersey accent to my wife. But I don't tell Des about all that.

He gives me a ton of direction and notes about the material, direction and notes that I can simplify as, "Don't do too much." The show is written very truthfully, and Des doesn't want his actors to push at all. They are to play the material simply and truthfully. This advice seems obvious, but must be very difficult to do when you are in the midst of a loud, rocking musical! The tendency is to want to rise to that level of energy. But that is not this show. That is not *Jersey Boys*. So I take the advice, thank everyone for seeing me again, and go back to real life.

At this point I realize, even though I have done a lot of work on this show, there is still more preparation I can do. I remember overhearing a conversation at my last audition in which an actor talked about being called in for a second dance call. What if that was me? I'd be in trouble.

So I call a friend who is an amazing Broadway dancer and has auditioned for *Jersey Boys* at least once before. I ask David Villella, "David, if I buy you some pizza, will you help me write down the combinations from the *Jersey Boys* audition?"

"Sure. Are you going in again for it?"

"No. I just want to write down the combinations."

"You want to write down the combinations even though you're not going in for another audition?"

"Well, I might be going in for another audition. If they call me."

"But they haven't called you yet?"

"No."

"But you want to write down the combinations?"

"Yes."

To a real dancer, my idea is unnecessary and perhaps a tad obsessive. But David agrees to help me anyway because he is a terrific guy. He visits me that week and we piece together the two dance combinations from memory. I write down every single move so that I can re-learn the dances on my own if the need arises.

*　　　　　　*　　　　　　*

Another month goes by before I am called in for a "work session." I am told this session will be a rehearsal to prep me for my next meeting with Des. I guess they still like me for this role. So I go through the morning preparation again and show up ready to tweak my performance. I've been working hard on keeping things simpler, and I've been trying to develop a voice for the character. My regular speaking voice sits rather high and resonates through my nose. It's nasally. I find strength in a character, in part, by adjusting my voice down to a deeper chest resonance. This was one major change I made before attending the work session…and I am quickly told that it is no good. Richard Hester, who has seen a hundred guys go through this process, recommends that I find the truth of Tommy in my own voice, that the choice I made is, quite simply, too fake. It hurts to hear because I am having a hard time finding the truth in my version of this character, and I thought I had found a vocal choice that could help.

The session ends with me feeling somewhat disheartened. The only positive thing is that, once again, I am the only Tommy present at the studio this day. From all outside impressions, there are far fewer guys in the mix to play Tommy than there are for the other roles.

The next day I get a call. Merri Sugarman says she appreciates the work I did yesterday and now they would like me to come to…another dance audition!

What?! Can you imagine how proud I feel to have prepared for this very possibility?

Can you imagine how grateful I now feel for David Villella? I spend a week re-learning the combinations from my notes and go to that audition ready as ever. The combinations are exactly as I remember and, even though I am not a good dancer, I make it through with dignity. Sergio, the choreographer, is at this audition and he watches me a few times. His note: "Just chill out." Ha, that's great! He doesn't say, "You don't know what you're doing." He doesn't say, "You look like a monkey." He says, "Just chill out." I cannot possibly chill out. I am far too wound up and sweaty to chill out. But at least it's not a horrible note. And it puts me in a terrific mood for my wedding...

You may kiss the bride...

©Daniel Robert Sullivan

*   *   *

On May 18th, 2008 Cara and I are married under a brilliantly white gazebo near the harbor in Newport, Rhode Island. Waves roll in gently not fifteen feet from our guests, the majority of whom stand around the perimeter of sea-aged pillars holding up the roof. A handful of chairs form an aisle and hundreds of buoyed sailboats provide a backdrop. The ceremony is simple, written by us and performed by our friend Jessica who was internet-ordained for this very purpose. Cara looks stunning in a slightly retro and very backless dress, and I look adequate in pants that are much too tight in the crotch. Cousins Mindy and Laura help decorate. Uncle Frank takes pictures. And Cara, Mark, Rachel, and I hold hands as we declare ourselves a brand new family.

Our reception is held in an old vaudeville theatre. Now used as a movie house, the Jane Pickens Theater can fly in a screen over its footlight-ringed stage. With a screen and a stage available, Cara and I were compelled to create a movie and a show.

The movie took two months to create, and tells the story of us planning our wedding together. Screening it at the very beginning of the reception sets the tone for the evening, for our movie bursts with funny family commentary, sentiment, and lots of jokes at my expense. One of the biggest laughs comes from a line I took directly from *Jersey Boys*, but stealing another writer's bit is not something my family can judge me for on my wedding day, right?

After eating, Cara and I host an old-time vaudeville show for our guests' entertainment. Having solicited our talented friends for acts, we have quite the production. Aaron and Shannon sing a romantic song together, after which Aaron wails on a great power ballad. Chris and Jenny perform "Who's On First?" in its entirety, having rehearsed it thirty times on the twelve-hour drive here. My new father-in-law, Fred, plays his fiddle, Cousin Emma sings a song she wrote herself, Cousin Brian dresses as John Lennon to give us a tune on his guitar, Dan and Sarah offer a Leonard Cohen piece and forget the words, Rachel sings from *Phantom of the Opera*, TJ kills with some stand-up, Ralph gives a toast in French, and Cara and I sing a fun duet about how we want to be "Rich, Famous, and Powerful." This is my favorite show that I've been a part of to date. At the end of the night, with the kids away with family, Cara and I fall into each other's arms and I have never been more content.

We honeymoon in an RV for two weeks, exploring Alaska together because it's the first affordable place we thought of that neither of us has visited. We get eaten by four-foot long mosquitoes, find $0.000012 while panning for gold, get horribly seasick a half-hour into an eight-hour cruise, witness bald eagles mating, and laugh when the RV's septic tank empties all over my shoes. Now, I am a guy who would normally freak out when something like this happens, but with Cara there it feels like I'm not allowed to be stressed. She gives me a slight smile, and the disaster becomes funny. I think that's why I like having her around.

*   *   *

More weeks go by. Driven by my new desire to prepare even more for these *Jersey Boys* auditions, I look online for a real rock 'n' roll vocal coach. I'm not an amazing singer, but I can do a good rock sound and feel it might serve me to sing with someone who specializes in this kind of thing. The guy I find has a list of singers he has worked with, all of which I have heard of. He coaches out of his apartment on the Upper West Side. I go there and am immediately impressed. The building is one of those old, gorgeous, block-long, pre-war buildings. The apartment resides on the corner and looks like it must be at least seven or eight rooms on the inside. I knock on the door with high expectations…and a short, hairy man wearing old sweat pants and holding a glass of whiskey opens the door. It is 11:00 a.m. and I know I am about to have a good story.

He leads me into his "studio," which is a cramped room filled with speakers, keyboards, and broken guitars piled to the ceiling. He is definitely drunk. He asks me what I am here for and I show him a couple of songs from *Jersey Boys*. He perks up at this, and pulls out a CD. The CD is his band's first, he says, and was recorded back in the 60s. He tells me to look at the picture of him on the back cover and see if I can recognize the guy standing next to him. Well, I'll be damned if the guy next to him isn't Bob Crewe, the Four Seasons' writer/producer and a major character in *Jersey Boys*. Bob Crewe produced this guy's album. Ok, maybe this is going to work out after all!

So, the drunken man (who shall continue to remain nameless so that he doesn't sue me when this book comes out) begins to play my music. I tell him something is wrong, that I think he might be playing in the wrong key. He insists I am incorrect, and tells me to sing along. I sing, and am now quite sure it is the wrong key. I may not be a musical expert, but I've been rehearsing in this key for a year and I know if something is not played in it.

34

After singing his way a couple of times, I notice that his keyboard has a giant screen on the top of it saying that it is in "automatic transposing" mode, changing the song to a different key than what his fingers are actually playing. I told you so.

After a quick break (yes, a break after only fifteen minutes) during which I suspect he had another drink, this guy starts giving me his advice.

"You gotta yell this shit!" he says. "This is rock and roll! The people wanna feel your power; they wanna feel your throat rip apart!"

Did I mention I was singing "Earth Angel?" Now, this song may technically be considered early rock and roll, but I certainly don't think that 50's singers were ripping their throats apart when they sang it. This guy is a loon, so I am very ready to leave when my hour is up. And my throat hurts for the rest of the day.

*   *   *

Later in the week I realize that, with all my preparation for the technical aspects of these auditions, I have not yet researched the genesis of the show as a whole.

Jersey Boys began when a writer named Rick Elice was approached in 2002 about working on a reality-based project about the Four Seasons. Frankie Valli and Bob Gaudio were looking at a number of ideas: television movie, feature-length film, Broadway musical revue. These two original members of the band produced hundreds of pages of interview material with their version of life events. (Rumor has it that Tommy DeVito has an unpublished four-hundred page autobiography with his own version of everything, but *Jersey Boys* uses only Frankie and Bob's version.)

Rick Elice brought his friend and prospective writing partner, Academy Award-winning Marshall Brickman, along for an initial lunch meeting with Frankie and Bob, and each became enamored with the stories that were told. Yes, Frankie Valli started out as a kid too young to be allowed in the bars where they sang. Yes, Tommy DeVito got arrested multiple times while leading the band through their early years. Yes, Joe Pesci introduced Bob Gaudio to Frankie. Yes, somebody faked a murder in Frankie's car. Yes, the entire band spent a night in jail together because of an unpaid hotel bill. Yes, they all came

35

from the wrong side of the tracks and struggled together for ten long years before hitting it big with "Sherry." Yes, everyone in that part of town was connected to the mob. Yes, they removed Tommy from the group because of his gambling and tax debts. And yes, they are the only American group to have Top Ten hits before, during, and after the British Invasion. What great material!

So Rick Elice and Marshall Brickman created an outline for a potential show in a traditional musical theatre style (i.e. slightly fictionalized characters breaking out into song when the scene reaches its peak) and brought it to Dodger Properties, who in turn brought it to Des McAnuff, then Artistic Director of La Jolla Playhouse in California.

When Des read the outline, filled with these amazing band anecdotes that no one had really heard before, he promptly said... "No, thank you."

Apparently, Des would only work on this show if it was absolutely true and absolutely non-traditional. He wanted a biographical musical that placed the songs in real places: clubs, concerts, studio recordings. He wanted it told from each band member's slightly different point of view, and he wanted it done soon so he could run it at his theatre in eight months. As usual, Des got everything he wanted.

Jersey Boys opened at La Jolla on October 17th, 2004. It sold out every night. It transferred to Broadway, opening there on November 6th, 2005. It sold out every night there too. It opened a touring company on December 10th, 2006. It has since sold out every night. The rest is history. And I am hoping beyond hope that I become part of that history.

*   *   *

Over a year has gone by now since my first audition (one year, seven days, twelve hours, and fourteen minutes...not that I'm counting) and I am actually still feeling positive. I have been lucky finding work at small theatres in shows I care about, and have even been cast four times in one particularly wonderful play. *Almost, Maine* is a beautiful piece of work written by a guy who I now feel privileged to call a friend, John Cariani. His play has become a prominent feature in my life in the past year, as I have spent many months working on it in New Jersey, Connecticut, and upstate New York. I commute to these theatres by train, and spend much of the daily rides reviewing *Jersey Boys* material or listening to the cast album.

In a very minor way, I feel like I've hit my stride. I am teaching and lecturing a lot to make money, performing in many small theatres, booking a few voiceover spots, and going on many good auditions. I have a great apartment, an amazing family, and the potential for great things. I even have two upcoming shows lined up back-to-back with no downtime in between, something that has never happened to me before in my life. Two shows back-to-back, both with decent paychecks, means that I am able to pass on the Teaching Artist work for a while and live as a full-time actor. The next six months look great, and it all makes me feel quite fulfilled.

But this is 2008 in New York City, time of the housing crisis and the banking crisis and the unemployment crisis and all sorts of other crises that make small, non-profit theatres suffer. Within two days, I get two calls:

"Dan, that new musical you were supposed to play the lead in at Queens Theatre in the Park has been postponed indefinitely."

Then, "Dan, the new production of *Almost, Maine* you were supposed to start rehearsals for tomorrow at Stamford Theatre Works has been cancelled because the theatre went bankrupt."

And in one fell swoop, I have nothing on the calendar for six months and no source of income.

*   *   *

Having too much free time on my hands is not something I am used to or enjoy. The gestation period of becoming (trying to become) a Jersey Boy is coming within sight of the gestation period an African elephant (about twenty-three months).

Too much time passes. Work is scarce. Once again, the call comes in from Merri Sugarman's office that Des is coming to town the day after tomorrow and a job is available this time. And look how these things work out; I am free to attend now that I have absolutely nothing to do that day. I am told the first requirement of the audition day will be a new feature in the *Jersey Boys* casting roller coaster—a harmony audition. I am being sent some sheet music (which, if you recall, I can't really read) with four different harmony lines on it and an mp3 of those lines (thank goodness). So before appearing in front of Des with my Tommy material, I will be appearing in front of Ron Melrose and be asked to sing each of these four lines of music. And so, once again, my next two days are filled with learning new material. It's music for "Let's Hang On," a song in the show that Tommy doesn't even sing.

But, I rehearse the four bits over and over and over again until I know them and each one feels like its own song. Humming along to each of them a hundred times is the only way I know how to learn.

The day arrives and we are called in groups for the harmony audition. I know the parts well, but this proves to be a stressful audition. Ron assigns parts to sing at random, listens to each of us sing them, and then quickly changes the part assignments and listens to us sing the new ones in ever-changing groups of four. This continues for fifteen minutes, and the singers are either mastering it or really embarrassing themselves. Preparation counts in this kind of thing, and I have a feeling that is part of what Ron is looking for. But he also just needs to know that an actor can hold on to a tight harmony line. Some of the guys can barely hang on to their first part, never mind switch to a different one without a break in between.

I survive because of my preparation. Only once do I begin singing the wrong part. Ron notices right away (his ear is ridiculously aware), corrects me, and I am ok from then on. If this group is graded "pass" or "fail," I think about three-fourths of us pass and the rest, very clearly, fail. A couple of them fail big time.

Later in the day, I appear before Des again. There is always a team of people behind the table at these auditions, maybe fourteen people total, but Des takes the focus. He is a presence in every room. He dresses cool, has wild and unkempt hair, and a very distinctive voice. With his presence bearing down on me, I blast through all of my standard material: Elvis song, Tommy songs, and Tommy scenes. I am not in the calmest state-of-mind, as I now hope to book this show not just as the realization of a dream, but simply as a way to pay my rent. When I am through, Des has no notes or advice, but guilelessly thanks me for coming in and sends me on my way. This is not a good sign.

Sure enough, the next day I get a call from my agent, "Dan, this is not an offer yet, but they want to know if you would be at all interested in an ensemble role. They are not offering the role of Tommy." And to top it all off, my agent also tells me that *The Lion King* people have asked that I come in for a third callback for an ensemble role on the tour. Funny how things happen. Two years ago I would have jumped out of my pants (yes, my pants) at a call like this. An ensemble role in a worldwide smash-hit musical? Hell, yeah!

Now, I am a practical guy who is obsessed with budgeting and schedules. But I also have a gambling streak in me. And here my gambling streak shows its face. My agent and I decide that we should take the risk in turning down the two possibilities with the hope that something bigger will come along soon. We tell *The Lion King* people, "No, thank you," and the *Jersey Boys* people, "We are now only interested in the role of Tommy." A few days later, the stellar Michael Cunio is announced as the new Tommy in the Chicago Company of *Jersey Boys*, while I stand in line at 7:00 a.m. waiting to sign up for another general audition.

*   *   *

The life of a small-time actor requires an ever-present positive attitude. I am pretty sure my attitude towards auditioning, whether I book the job or not, must be showing through in these pages. I have a generally hopeful outlook; I wouldn't survive without one. The only reason I am not routinely damaged by being judged and passed over is that I am constantly looking forward to the next opportunity. I persistently remind myself that the person I am auditioning for today has no idea what I did in my audition for that other job yesterday.

Around this time I get close to being very lucky. I have a regular audition, one of many that week, that results in a callback. A callback is when I really kick things into gear, for that's when I know that I at least look like I could fit the role. The show is *The Story of My Life*. It is a very real, very touching musical that premiered in Canada and is coming to Broadway in a few months. It has only two actors, and they are looking to cast an understudy to cover both of them. (This would later change as they would end up casting two understudies, but at this point they want to find a guy who can do it all.)

Preparing for the callback, I get very familiar with the show and, of course, learn three songs and about twenty pages of the script. This musical floors me. It is amazing. (I think everything is amazing. People tell me that all the time. But this show really is.) I attend the callback and receive a second callback. I attend the second callback and am asked to come in for a work session with Richard Maltby, Jr., the director. I work very hard and spend many, many hours preparing for these callbacks and the final work session (I even have a bad cold, my first time being sick in two years), but in the end I do not book the job. The letdown with this kind of news, though I am very used to it, still stings. That night, I sit alone in my apartment and write the following journal entry as a sort of catharsis:

Nobody said it was going to be easy, but nobody said it was going to be this hard either.

We are talking about people who pursue a dream that probably began when they were ten years old, and who continue to pursue that dream for twenty, thirty, even forty years. Everything they do tailors to that pursuit.

Why are there so many actor/waiters? Because waiting tables is an evening job with flexibility and decent pay. Not because the actors can't do anything else, but because they are sacrificing money, a nice apartment, vacations, and going out to restaurants themselves, all in the pursuit of their one overarching dream. And it is a dream of theatre; a love of performing that drives them. They are not hoping for fame. They are hoping to be a nameless dancer in the ensemble. If they wanted fame, New York is certainly not the place to find it; there are too many people and too few opportunities here. They are not hoping for money. Ensemble roles on Broadway pay $1700 per week, and that is only for as long as the show runs. Remember that most shows close in months, and even steadily-working actors usually find themselves with a year between shows. These jobs do not create affluent actors. Nor do these jobs create recognizable actors. And yet thousands, yes, thousands of actors in this city dream about it when they sleep at night.

Here's a typical situation: an actor finds out that he has an audition next week for a small part on Broadway. He spends every night memorizing and rehearsing the nineteen pages of lines for the audition. He spends $40 to have someone play him the three new songs he needs to learn, and then $150 to meet with a vocal coach who

40

will help him sing them well. He takes the night before the audition off from any kind of work, and has to leave the entire next day free as well. He goes to bed early, then wakes up early because, physically speaking, the voice needs a few hours to warm up to peak performance. He auditions, then waits for a phone call. It comes, and he is asked to come back two days later for a callback. He then takes that day off work and repeats the routine. Excellent, another callback. He takes that day off work as well, and again repeats the routine. He waits for the call. By this time, it is so close he can taste it. He waits an hour. A few hours. An evening. A day. Finally, a call from his agent: they loved him; but he was too young. Or too old. Or not quite a good enough dancer. Or they wanted more of a tenor. Or anything. It doesn't matter because now he is sad. He'll get back that drive again, but remember that he has now dropped $190, three days of lost work, and countless rehearsal hours in pursuit of this possible job.

Alone, with nothing to do today, I nearly tear up. It felt so close. I may come this close again, sure. But it will be at least a year. And I tell myself that I am one of the lucky ones! I have an agent looking for these opportunities for me. Not all actors have that; in fact, most don't. I remember being onstage for the first time in fifth grade. I want to thank the teacher who put me there...but what would I thank her for? That I struggle to find work now? That she instilled in me an "unrealistic" dream? It doesn't matter if it's unrealistic, it won't go away! Why won't it go away? I could be a lot happier on a day-to-day basis if I had a steady job somewhere, with a nice house and health insurance. I could have those things. It is not that I am not smart. Or capable. I have a wonderful day job at a theatre company that treats me with respect and challenges me every day. But it is not what I have dreamed of since I put on the red tin soldier costume that Aunt Jill made me and proclaimed, "I'm Colonel Cuddly, at your service, dolls!" It is not the dream I had when I started crying with happiness (and I've never told anyone this until now) when I was cast in my first high school play as a freshman. So what if the part was small? It is not the dream I had when I

41

got my first lead role in a real theatre that actually paid me money. That role went to my head. It was a lesson. I thought everything would get easier after that role. It never got easier.

Every decision I've ever made has been influenced by this dream. Yes, every decision: wife, then ex-wife, cities, then new wife, kids. I missed my grandfather getting re-married because of a performance, and missed his funeral because of one as well. I carry the funeral card around with me because I feel so guilty, but really, would I have done anything different? I have been asked, "When are you going to give up?" I have been asked, "Do you think you'll ever get a real job?" But I have also been told, "I believe in you," and those are the words that get me up in the morning.

Today was a hard day. I trust tomorrow will be better.

*　　　　　　*　　　　　　*

I struggle to put together a full schedule of Teaching Artist work to fill my time, and I audition full-tilt, as usual. After a couple months looking for acting work, I am lucky to book two gigs back-to-back again. And they both look like they could be the most joyous gigs of my career. First, I will be in yet another production of *Almost, Maine*, but this time under the direction of the author, and my friend, John Cariani. This marks the first time he will direct his own play, and it should be quite special. Next, I will be spending the summer (along with my family) near my parents in Rhode Island, playing the lead in one of Theatre-By-The-Sea's summer musicals. The theatre's new producers are friends of mine, and I grew up working as an usher at that place. It feels like I am coming full-circle, and aunts, uncles, and cousins are already looking for their tickets.

I am content. It is a happy Thursday evening and I am having a burger in Midtown Manhattan with my friend from Theatre-By-The-Sea. An hour later I will meet up with John Cariani to see a play he invited me along to. During dinner, I receive a call from my agent. This is unusual; since it is past normal business hours, I figure it is just updated information about a small audition coming up. Being in the middle of dinner, I let the call go to voicemail. When the bill is paid, but before leaving the restaurant, I listen to the voicemail and my jaw drops.

"Dan, they are looking for a replacement for the role of Tommy in the Toronto production of *Jersey Boys* and they need to see you for a work session first thing tomorrow morning."

The long-running shows in Toronto are like the Broadway of Canada. Toronto is only an hour plane ride away; this could work. This is happening tomorrow morning. But it means I would have to quit the two jobs I now have booked; two jobs that not only mean a lot to me, but that were given to me by the very people I am hanging out with tonight. Oh boy.

After a couple of very understanding conversations, my friends assure me that there will be no hard feelings if I do have to quit these jobs, for who could say no to *Jersey Boys*? This is calming to hear, but really I can't even believe I am having these conversations in the first place.

I go home, review the scenes and songs, and prepare for the next day's routine.

*   *   *

The work session is stressful. It is just Merri Sugarman, Richard Hester, and me alone in the Dodger's rehearsal space. Dodger Properties is the producing organization behind *Jersey Boys*, and countless other hit shows. Their offices take up part of a floor near 8th Avenue and 43rd Street in Manhattan, and their private rehearsal space takes up the rest of the floor. It is a beautiful space with pictures of current and older shows on the walls. I am dressed well, warmed up, and ready to go, when Richard begins the session by asking me, "So, do you know what happened last time?"

Um. Nope.

"Dan, for whatever reason, the last time you were here you just did too much. You were wound up, putting on too much of a fake voice, and just not the Tommy we first saw." Ouch.

So we work for an hour dissecting each scene and go through exactly what Des is looking for. Richard is good at this. He opens my eyes to things and directs me as if I already have the role and am preparing to perform. He smoothes down my Tommy into a calmer character. He amps up the jokes by telling me it is ok to find a little enjoyment in intimidating the other characters. He tells me it is good for Tommy to make fun of himself in the final monologue, for Tommy knows that he looks a bit

43

pathetic from the outside. But also that I must defend myself in the last couple sentences, convincing everyone that things are not really as pathetic as they appear. If I knew a year ago all the things Richard is telling me today, I would be doing the show already. Damn it! He psyches me up, and makes me think I can get this.

Richard and Merri tell me to come back on Sunday. They tell me that Frankie Valli and Bob Gaudio will be there, so as not to let it surprise me. They have a debate about whether I should wear the suit I have worn all along, or a more casual outfit. They settle on the suit. They are trying to show me off.

The next day is a blur of final at-home rehearsals. On Sunday morning, I begin my pre-audition routine again, interrupting it only because I am inspired to start writing things down. And that's where this book really begins…

*   *   *

April 26th, 2009

It is a Sunday morning. I am sitting at my kitchen counter in Manhattan and I've just decided that the stuff I am feeling right now could make a good book. The journey I start later this afternoon might be of interest to a lot of people: actors, students, dreamers. Today is my final audition for the leading role of Tommy DeVito in *Jersey Boys: The Story of Frankie Valli and the Four Seasons*. I have been a struggling professional actor for all of my adult life, and this job (God, I hope I get it) will be the only high profile one I have ever had. *Jersey Boys* is a worldwide phenomenon, and this will not only be my big break, but the fulfillment of a dream I have had since Mrs. King cast me in my first musical in the fifth grade.

My hands are trembling. I inherited this nervous trait from my mother, although today the trembling is compounded by the vast amount of coffee I drank while running over my lines one last time. It's been almost two years since my first audition for *Jersey Boys*. The one today will be lucky number thirteen.

THE FINAL AUDITION

CLASSIC LAS VEGAS, MEDICINAL BANANAS, & DES McANUFF'S COLOGNE

April 26th, 2009

The audition is once again at the Dodger's rehearsal studio, that beautifully sunlit room on 43rd Street. This feels right. I am able to go in already focused and ready to do exactly as I rehearsed the other day. Of course, on Friday there were only two other people in the room; today there are almost a thousand.

Michael David is here. He is the famous producer in charge of Dodger Properties. An iconic theatre personality, he is instantly recognizable by his long, full beard. This beard is the first thing I see when I walk in the room. It is a fuzzy beacon of power.

Frankie Valli is here. He really is a small man, in size and attitude. For a guy who has influenced the world of music (and theatre) so much over the past fifty years, I must admit that I expected a stronger presence. But he is humble. He is soft-spoken. He comes out of the room ten minutes before my audition and asks where to find the bathroom. He wears all black, and sports a gold watch and earring. He looks like classic Las Vegas. And his hair is the same as it has always been—big and round.

Bob Gaudio is here…or so I'm told. I can't see him. Knowing the way the show portrays Bob (quietly in control, out of the spotlight), I guess I shouldn't be surprised that he becomes lost in the sea of faces. He does not introduce himself, nor does anyone else introduce him. I suppose he just watches from the back of the room, exerting his control later, in private.

Merri is here. Richard is here. Tara Rubin (Merri's boss) is here. Many interns are here. And all of these people feel like my cheering section. I feel like they are on my side, like they are rooting for me. I have never felt this kind of energy in a casting session before in my life. And Des is here. Of course. He asks me to play guitar and I bust out my trusty, "That's All Right, Mama." Richard told me that Des prefers his guitar players to look up at the audience when accompanying themselves, instead of looking down at the fret board. Des plays guitar well, so he should know how hard this is to do! But I practiced, and I commit.

"That's good, Dan. Now can you do the first scene?"

The reader the casting office brought is someone I have never seen at a *Jersey Boys* audition before. But I know him! We performed together once before and he was also a reader on the last job I booked. He is good, really committing to the material. He isn't as off-book for the scenes as I have become accustomed to, but I consider this a good sign; it shows me that he hasn't been doing these same scenes all day long. I am unique. Hopefully I am the only Tommy being seen today. All signs look good.

I perform the first Tommy-Frankie scene, the one that establishes their big brother-little brother relationship. There is a set of keys used in this scene, and for the first time I actually bring a set to pull out of my pocket. This was a great debate for me, whether to bring real keys or not. See, an actor traditionally doesn't want to bring props with him to an audition. It isn't necessary, and can sometimes make him look a bit crazy. (I won't get into the story of my audition for *Avenue Q*—the audition for which I purchased two $100 puppets, thinking it might make me stand out. Oh, I stood out all right. And I was never called in for *Avenue Q* again.) I decide, though, that the keys are a small enough prop, and the scene is sufficiently grounded in reality, that adding them will actually help me.

Genetics could ruin this though, for holding out the keys to Frankie might reveal my little inherited quirk of trembling hands. In preparation for this, I ate three bananas. I read somewhere that bananas are calming to the nervous system. (If anyone knows otherwise, please don't tell me. They work for me today [even if only psychologically], and I plan on using this technique again!)

The scene goes well, and I am asked to perform the next one. The next scene in the packet is more of a bullying scene, for it involves Tommy exerting his control over Joe Pesci. (Yeah, that Joe Pesci.) After we are finished, Des rises from his throne and comes over to talk to me privately. This is presented as a very special, very fatherly moment. Des puts his arm around me like a football coach about to whisper to his player. It is manly, but intimate. His cologne is very strong. He guides me to the back of the room. Respectfully, everyone else pretends to busy themselves. But guess what? The studio is very small and they are all right there on the other side of the table hearing every word that is spoken. Des tells me a bunch of stuff—brilliant stuff—which I have to filter into something I can actually show him in five seconds. My edited version of what he says: "smile more." So I do. And he laughs.

After that, I do the infamous hit-on-the-reporter scene with Merri. Since I began the audition process, casting performers for this show seems to have become Merri's full-time job. Thus, she is now very much off-book.

I perform the final monologue, and it is received with what appears to be quiet contentment. I receive absolutely no more notes, so either Des loves what I am doing and is convinced I can do the part, or he's given up.

I leave the room offering much appreciation, and as I am putting my guitar back into its case, another guy is called in to read for Tommy. He is the last actor auditioning this day. Often, being the last actor seen is a sign that you are preferred. I hope he is not preferred.

I leave the studio, call my wife to tell her how it went, and begin walking home in the first 90° day of the year. I am wearing my dark suit and black shirt, and am carrying my heavy guitar case and a backpack full of music and hair products. I am so worked up, because of the day, the heat, and my baggage, that I have to stop in a little park to calm myself down. (Ok, "park" is an exaggeration. I am in front of Macy's on a bench with a two-foot by four-foot patch of brown grass behind me.)

When I finally arrive home, I go through one last audition routine, a routine that I carry out after each round of *Jersey Boys* calls. I put away my large book of audition music in our bedside drawer, stick the audition scenes into their manila envelope in my backpack, put my guitar strap back on the electric guitar where it usually lives, hang my Ovation back on the wall, place my guitar tuner and picks back in their place next to the television, and carry the guitar case down to our basement storage cage (stuffing it in with all my might because we really have too much stuff in that storage cage). I am done, for now.

I go to the small gym in our building. No one's there (it's the middle of the day, and most people are working), so I have my phone out and the ringer on high. I am not sure when I will receive a call, and I don't want to miss it. After a

47

quick workout, I take a long walk, leaving the phone in my hand and the ringer on high. I do some paperwork for an upcoming workshop I am teaching, and leave the phone next to my computer with the ringer on high. Cara comes home and we have a bit of drama with Mark and some teenage shenanigans that occurred on a recent Boy Scout trip, but I leave my phone out while we talk to him (yup, ringer on high). We have a family dinner out at Blockhead's, a terrific Mexican restaurant with cheap and delicious margaritas, and I leave the phone next to the salsa with the ringer still very much on high.

No calls come today. I guess I have one more night to dream.

PREPARING TO LEAVE

TO-DO LISTS, DRAMATURGICAL LECTURES, & DANGEROUS BUTTERFLIES

April 27, 2009

The phone rings this morning at 9:40 a.m. It's Meg; I answer it as calmly as I can manage. Cara just about jumps out of her pants when the phone rings; and it is hard to focus when your hot wife is jumping out of her pants. But Meg just wants to check in and see how the audition went. I tell her it went well enough, and leave the details for her to read about if this book ever gets published.

At 10:30 a.m., the phone rings again. I sit down on the couch before answering, knowing this has to be news—good or bad. Before even saying hello, Meg whispers, "Dan, you got it."

I got it.

I actually got it.

Cara crawls onto the couch next to me and is hardly controlling herself. I say, "Oh. My. God." Cara jumps up with a squeal, and I start thinking of all the million-and-a-half things I now need to do. Why can't I just live in the moment like our therapist (yes, our therapist) says I should?

The first thing Meg tells me is that I should send Merri Sugarman a nice bouquet of flowers. I am thinking, "And one for you, too, I believe." But the truth is I had already planned to send Merri some kind of thank you today anyway; this thank you will just be a bit more lavish.

Meg has no details for me yet, but my mind is revving with a to-do list. I actually start writing these chores down while I am still on the phone with her because there is much to be done and I only have a half-hour before I have to leave for a meeting at the Roundabout.

In the next blur of thirty minutes, I assign Cara the task of picking out the perfect flowers to send to Merri and Meg. (She has a much better eye than I for these things, and confirming this, Merri later calls me a "class act" for sending such a nice ensemble. Well done, Cara!) I call my mother, who has to bottle her excitement because she is among patients at work. I send a text to my brother, and he replies that I am "gonna b famous." (I text back that I am "scared shtlss.") I email my stepfather at work, but my mother called him already during the two minutes I spent texting. I call my producing friend at Theatre-By-The-Sea and he knows instantly what I am going to say. My agent will make an official call to him soon, but I wanted to reach him first. And I call John Cariani to bow out of his production of *Almost, Maine*. This one's tricky. I am very afraid of burning bridges, and I really want to maintain a friendship with this well-known guy. He takes the news well enough, and asks for recommendations for someone who can take my place.

Then I have to run to my meeting! Boy, there is never time to just sit down and appreciate things, is there? Toward the end of the meeting I begin helping with the daunting task of re-assigning all of the workshops, classes, and lectures I was to give over the next few months. The projects I work on with Roundabout are many and varied, but today my job is to quit all of the following:

- Twenty classroom workshops at Manhattan Bridges High School centering on lyric writing for musical theatre.
- Ten classroom workshops at IS 237 Middle School in Queens using Set Design to teach Math skills.
- Many hours of work as the project coordinator for the Roundabout's partnership with the Brooklyn School for Music and Theater.
- Ten classroom workshops at IS 237 Middle School using tableaus and storytelling to expand ESL skills.
- Fifteen private Professional Development workshops dealing with arts integration with a new English teacher at the Brooklyn School for Music and Theater.
- An entire, three-month series of dramaturgical lectures at the Roundabout's new production of *Waiting for Godot*.
- Ten workshops for high school students and their teachers to introduce them to the themes addressed in *Waiting for Godot*.

50

After many hours of re-organizing these projects, I return home and, as is the modern thing to do, update my Facebook status with my news and a comment that "dreams really do come true." Truer words have never been spoken. With this job, I feel like my oldest dream is *almost* coming true. Almost. My dream has always been to star in a Broadway show. Now I will be starring in a Broadway show…in Canada. Ok. It's close. And can I even dare to dream that it will be a gigantic stepping-stone to actually starring on Broadway? Yup. I will dare to dream that.

My Facebook status inspires about sixty people to write their congratulations, and about twenty people to call me. My phone rings so much I can't keep up. I am exhausted with thoughts and plans, and I don't even know when I'll be starting rehearsal yet. I have no details and no idea when the details will be revealed. My agent says they are talking about sending me to rehearse with the National Tour of the show, or maybe with the Chicago Company. And Cara and I have to figure out whether we will all be able to spend the summer together in Toronto (we have to, we just have to) and to get plane tickets to…where?

Today is the glamour part of getting the job: the excitement, the phone calls, the spreading of good news. Tomorrow will bring the work: the planning, the schedules, the memorizing. I have a feeling I'm going to be exhausted for weeks to come.

And did I mention that, as I write this, I am starting to get pretty nervous? How am I going to pull off this cocky character? How am I going to learn all that choreography? I suck at choreography. Kick, ball-change.

April 28th, 2009

Meg said she would call as soon as she knew some dates, and today passes without a call coming in. As silly as it is, I start fearing something happened to the guy I am supposed to replace and he's decided to stay on in the show. That guy is Jeremy Kushnier, by the way. He is a stellar performer who originated the lead role of Ren in the Broadway production of *Footloose*. I saw him many times in that one. I also saw him in the Broadway production of *Rent* and a Kansas City production of *Jesus Christ Superstar*. I think he totally rocks and I will never, ever be able to compare. To top it all off, he's been doing *Jersey Boys* for two years now in various companies, so he's leaving gargantuan shoes for me to fill.

Why is he leaving anyway? My bet at this point is that he has been cast in either a Canadian television show or a new Broadway musical. Those would be good reasons to leave. Whatever the reason, I will be sloppy seconds to Jeremy Kushnier any day.

I spend all day doing more of the transition work involved in leaving the Roundabout. I meet with the different Teaching Artists who will be replacing me, go over notes and plans, and lead a few final workshops myself. This has all been surprisingly emotional for me. While I am realistic enough to know that I will probably be back teaching for them again next year, I find myself hoping that I will not be, and that makes leaving difficult. I love the people there. They are incredible artists.

I am kind of freakin' out! I am stressed because I want to organize the next year of our life, but I don't have enough information to do that yet. And my wife wants to go out to dinner. She is waiting for me in the other room right now. But I am incredibly tired. And I have to learn lines. I am thinking of buying this big *Jersey Boys* coffee table book from Barnes & Noble just so I have something I can start learning lines from. Isn't that crazy? I should just get an official script before I start rehearsal, but I am too embarrassed to ask for one.

And Cara wants to leave. Like, now. "Hon, what are you doing?" she asks from behind the door.

"I am pouring my angst-ridden thoughts into a journal."

"Can we go eat?" she wonders, with no impatience in her voice. Yet.

"Yeah. Let me just write down what you're saying right now."

"You're writing down what I'm saying right now? Why?"

"To inspire others to follow their dreams, regardless of the obstacles set before them."

"Am I an obstacle?" she asks.

"Well, right now you are. But only a little."

52

"How am I an obstacle?"

"Because I can't go out to dinner until I finish writing today's entry, and I can't finish writing today's entry until this conversation is over."

She is silent. I guess this conversation is over.

I get a little snarky when I'm stressed out. Sarcasm helps me lighten the burden. Good luck dealing with me tonight, my darling.

April 29th, 2009

Here we go. Meg calls today at 5:00 p.m. saying that I will start rehearsing this coming Tuesday. That is six days from now. Six days! Now I'm really freaking out.

My rehearsal/travel schedule will be a bit insane. Apparently, I will rehearse in New York for three days, fly to Toronto for a day to see the show, fly to Orlando to rehearse with the National Tour for two weeks, fly back to New York for a week of fittings, and then fly up to Toronto for two weeks before opening on June 16th. At least that is what they say now. Everything is subject to change, and I have many nervous butterflies in my stomach. Big butterflies. With razor-sharp wings.

I decide today that I need to have the script as soon as possible, so I go to Barnes & Noble to buy the coffee table book. The first two stores I try don't have it in stock, so by the time I reach the third store I have walked exactly fifty blocks, listening to the *Jersey Boys* cast recording the entire way. As if the album isn't thrilling enough, now I am picturing myself singing the songs and I get rammed full of excitement.

I pay a whopping $45 for the book—all because I am too timid to ask for a script in advance. So now I will be learning lines for my blockbuster musical debut out of a giant picture book.

I later learn that Jeremy Kushnier is leaving the Toronto cast because his wife (who also used to be in the show) is pregnant and they want to have the baby back in New York. So it's not a new Broadway musical or some television show causing him to leave *Jersey Boys*, it's just life. His wife is fierce, and he is a rock star. I have a feeling that baby will be fronting a band by the age of seven.

April 30th, 2009

Ready and rocking! I say my goodbyes at the Roundabout office, and compose an email to send to the various Teaching Artists I worked with there, all of whom are scattered around the city in their own pursuits. (No more than two of us ever seem to be in the same place at the same time.) The email kind of sums up my thoughts about the teaching portion of my life, so I'll reproduce it here:

> *Dear Roundabout Colleagues,*
>
> *It is with sadness and excitement, and more sadness and more excitement, that I must bid you all a temporary goodbye. I will be moving to Toronto, Canada in just a few days to join the cast of Jersey Boys as Tommy DeVito. While I am sure I will be back at Roundabout eventually, I fear that I would regret not saying a few words of "see you later" if I do not say them now.*
>
> *Without a doubt, Roundabout has been my artistic home for years now. How many people in this world are blessed to work at something they love (teaching artistry), and be encouraged there to pursue something else they love (acting)? It is no exaggeration to say that my work at Roundabout has enabled me to pursue my childhood dream of performing in large-scale jukebox musicals...*
>
> *Ok, maybe my childhood dream was not as specific as that, but you get the point.*
>
> *I have found more talented, dream-supporting people at Roundabout than anywhere else in the world. I have loved my time here. I am always wowed by our core group of Teaching Artists, and I am always envious of the creative brain-power of our leaders. I will miss seeing you all on those rare and wonderful times when we get to come together. And I will probably feel dumb for writing all this if the show closes and I am back here in September. If you're*

54

ever in Canada, drop by and let me take you out to dinner. I'll
be up there living a dream...and probably giving
dramaturgical talks in the lobby.

–Dan Sullivan

Though, I still have two more workshops to teach tomorrow, and a few months of paperwork that will be coming, the bulk of my work at this place is now complete.

I receive my official offer from the Canadian producers, and lots of detailed information along with it. For rehearsals in Orlando, I am given the choice of two hotels: one across from Walt Disney World, and the other ten miles away from it. I think I should go with the one ten miles away, just so that I am not tempted with distractions! I will have to be quite focused, I'm sure.

I email two people today for advice: Buck, my audition buddy and current *Jersey Boys* National Tour cast member, and Dean, my accountant. Buck speaks highly of the family atmosphere *Jersey Boys* has created, and congratulates me on finally getting in. Dean tells me some steps to take to let certain expenses be regarded as out-of-town travel business deductions.

Working in another country will be a bit tricky to keep track of, business-wise. For one, Canada regards actors as self-employed business entities, unlike the United States where actors are usually regular employees. And being a non-resident, there will be some tax withheld from my paycheck, but not the full amount I will actually owe; so I will need to make sure to set money aside for April 15th. My paycheck will be in Canadian dollars, so that leaves a whole other layer of confusion with our very specific budget.

And, to be brutally honest, my salary will not be as much as I expected. Granted, it is still more money than I have ever made from a theatre in my life, but their initial offer is not quite as dramatic a number as I would have hoped for. Know that the amount per week is much more than the union's minimum, but it still isn't life changing money, and much of it will be sequestered by the airlines when I fly home as often as possible in an attempt to maintain some semblance of family life. I shouldn't be complaining; it is a very generous number. I guess I was just dreaming too big.

I am writing this while waiting for three loads of laundry to dry. I figure I should wash everything now before things get even busier. I also need to make sure that I have lots of dance rehearsal clothes to sweat in. I haven't had a sweaty dance rehearsal in quite a long time. Oh! And I need to buy new sneakers. I will probably be wearing sneakers in rehearsal and my running shoes are so old that there's a good chance my baby toe might pop out of them any day now.

May 1st, 2009

Contract negotiations finish and it all becomes official. Truth be told, there weren't too many negotiations to be had. What am I going to do, say "No" if they don't give me enough money? They could pay me minimum wage and I would still find a way to make it work. (Of course, I don't tell them this.)

The contract says the producers will give me a place to live in Toronto for a month, but after that I will be on my own. I know this may become tax deductible, but renting a place will still make my salary drop even further. However, some minor perks in my first big contract: my own dressing room, a plane ticket for my wife to come up for my opening night, a small raise after six months, and four free tickets. That's four free tickets, period. Not four per show or four per month or four per year. Four. Period.

And my contract is for a year. This is just starting to set in. One year. I'm sure my family will be able to join me for the summer, but the school year is a different story. If I think too long about this right now I will start to get really sad. Traveling out of town for a theatre job is something that I think most actors would agree is inherently detrimental to a relationship. I have met very few couples that can survive it for long. Cara and I are very proactive in working to keep our relationship strong (so is our therapist), but it will not be easy to manage this separation. I'm already thinking too much about it.

Momentarily taking my mind off the long distance, I speak to a great guy at the Dodger's production office. Jeff sets up my rehearsal schedule (so scary) and tells me I will be his job for the next month. I've never been anybody's job for more than an hour (the dentist), so being somebody's job for an entire month seems a bit ridiculous. He will work with me on flight reservations, rehearsal locations, rental cars, and the like for all the cities to which I will be traveling. I think his job title is "Assistant Production Coordinator," and he is my first *Jersey Boys* friend.

Tomorrow, I get to go to the August Wilson Theatre to see the Broadway Company's wardrobe supervisor and try on some shirts. The bulk of my clothes, however, will be custom made by a tailor. And that, my friends, is awesome. I have never had a tailor-made suit before, and now I think I am going to have at least four!

Oh, and I chose the hotel near Disney World after all. How can I turn that down? I love Disney World.

May 2nd, 2009

Today is all about the clothes. I stop by the August Wilson and check in at the stage management office just like I had while seeing the show last year. I should be feeling more secure this time around, seeing as I have now booked the job, but I must admit I'm feeling just as intimidated as the first time. I have zero confidence when it comes to anything related to Broadway. I have a great work ethic, and I can convince people by faking confidence, but there is usually nothing genuine behind it.

The production stage manager gives me directions on how to get to the wardrobe room, directions that include four left turns, three right turns, a staircase, a tunnel, and a revolving bookcase. Needless to say, I get lost in the basement of the theatre. It is a maze down there. For anyone who might imagine Broadway dressing rooms, hair rooms, and wardrobe rooms to be glamorous, I can attest that they most certainly are not. They are basement rooms, musty, damp, and lit with the same type of fluorescent tubes that Tom Wingfield rails against. I find my way thanks to a small group of stagehands watching TV, and I introduce myself to the wardrobe department.

"Hello. I'm Daniel Robert Sullivan. Is this the wardrobe department?"

"Yes, it is. You're Daniel?"

"Yes. I'm Daniel."

"You're blond."

57

Are there no blond Italians? And is it really possible to tell a person's heritage based on their hair anyway? Aren't Irish guys and Italian guys the same on the inside? If you prick us, do we not bleed?

My visit here, it turns out, is quite simple. I have to try on some white shirts from Express to find the correct size. They are then going to buy a few of the shirts and dye them to the light purple color the Four Seasons wear through much of Act One. Also, I have to be measured for the only suit worn that is purchased off the rack. The suit is a black Calvin Klein, and I will wear it for "Rag Doll" and "Who Loves You."

Next, I have to go to be measured for the rest of my suits. In addition to the Calvin Klein, I will wear four other suits, all of which will be made by the famous St. Laurie Merchant Tailors on 32nd Street in Manhattan. This place is, quite literally, steps from my apartment—so I arrive for my appointment nice and early. I am greeted by the owner and his son, and am asked to wait just a few minutes while they get their paperwork together. While waiting, I check out their wall of photographs. In addition to *Jersey Boys* photos, there are pictures of Leonardo DiCaprio in Revolutionary Road, Denzel Washington in Malcolm X, and other stars that I would like to be friends with. These tailors are the real deal.

When the owner returns, he tells me that I am the first fair-haired Tommy he has seen. (Really, this again?) I ask him how many Tommys he has built suits for and he can't even count. Building for *Jersey Boys*, he says, has been a full-time business since 2006. Let's do some math; there are four lead characters, each with four suits. Each lead character has two understudies, and there is an additional actor who plays Frankie Valli for the matinees. That makes thirteen sets of four suits apiece, for a total of fifty-two suits per company. There are now seven companies throughout the world. That makes three hundred and sixty-four suits for the original lead actors in each company. But there have also been replacement actors in each company, like me. I'm guessing here, but I think about twenty-five replacement guys came into the show in the last couple of years. That makes another hundred suits, for a total of four hundred and sixty-four. And guess what? That doesn't take into account the ensemble.

Now the cost: if each suit for the lead actors costs, conservatively, $4000 to make from scratch, then St. Laurie Merchant Tailors has brought in $1,856,000 from *Jersey Boys* alone. And again, that is just for the lead actors. There are ensemble actors that need suits, too. And more companies opening soon. Unbelievable.

The father-son team taking my measurements is extremely well dressed; in fact, every employee in the place looks impeccable. I guess you have to if you work in a fancy suit-shop, but this is all new to me. The best suit I ever bought was from Men's Wearhouse. (They said I would like the way I looked, and they guaranteed it.) I bought my wedding suit online, another off the rack at Macy's, and have a hand-me-down winter suit from my uncle, which was given to me when I was a sophomore in high school and is still very much a part of my wardrobe.

After taking measurements, the gentleman helping asks me to try on a mock-up pair of pants. I go into the small dressing area, remove my shoes, and realize that both of my socks have holes in them. Big holes. Like, each big toe is sticking completely out of the sock. I am too embarrassed to come out of the dressing room like that, so I try to pull the holes down underneath my feet. Arranging the sock in a way that would look somewhat normal takes some time, far more time than I should have been taking just to try on a pair of pants. One of the employees asks if I am ok in there, I say I am fine, and I shuffle out. I have to shuffle, of course, because if I lift my feet at all then the sock will flip out and expose my little trick.

I am rescued a moment later, thank goodness. They notice that I am not wearing shoes and ask if I could go back and put them on. They like to see how the pants fall on the shoes. Nice. I should have known that.

May 3rd, 2009

I've been at home nearly all day learning lines from that big ol' picture book again. The print is small and impossible to highlight, so the memorizing job proves more difficult than I am used to. But it is still nice to know I am getting a jump-start on things.

Michael Lomenda, Jeff Madden, Quinn VanAntwerp, Daniel Robert Sullivan
©Joan Marcus

I am a firm believer in knowing all, or at least most, of my lines before beginning rehearsals. Every actor differs in this regard, but because I rely so much on the physical side of acting (like how a character moves and speaks) I find I cannot dive into the work until the script is out of my hand. It will be some time before I know the lines cold, but it is nice going into the first set of rehearsals with some idea of what words to say.

Learning lines is a skill that takes practice, but I believe that non-actors often place too much emphasis on the task. "I don't know how you guys remember all of those lines!" is a comment actors hear often. But it is really no different than knowing the words to hundreds of songs that you sing along with in your car. Both scripts and sing-a-longs require repetition, nothing more.

I sit with the *Jersey Boys* script for a total of seven hours today, and I probably only learn about three new scenes. I speak the words a hundred times or more, talking back to the book while my hand covers the next line.

But still, only three new scenes are in my brain. There is no mystery to the skill of memorizing lines. It just takes time.

Whenever I start getting sleepy, as is bound to happen when sitting in one place staring at the same five pages of a book, I try to do something to wake myself up. I make a quick trip to the gym this morning to do just that, and come back with fresh eyes. The next time I begin nodding, I remember reading that while in rehearsals John Lloyd Young, the original and Tony Award-winning Frankie Valli, used to swim every day just to keep up his stamina for the draining hours of choreography and singing. Immediately, I decide that I should do the same. But I don't have a pool. So I grab my new sneakers and go for a run, and I come back again with fresh eyes and a brain that is ready to remember. I think I should vow to do this every day until I open the show, if only so I can be like Tony Award-winning John Lloyd Young. Who wouldn't want to be like Tony Award-winning John Lloyd Young?

Even though I have been busy working on lines, it is very nice to be home with Cara. She sits silently by my side while I study; building up time together before I head out, I guess. (She remains by my side as I pause to write today's entry.) Late in the afternoon, she tries to work out some plans for her and the kids this summer. It is a frustrating puzzle for her, what with grandparent visits, summer camp, and school letting out late this year for one child and starting earlier next year for the other. And Cara feels, as I do, that we won't be able to start dealing with our separation until we know exactly where everyone will be for the next six months or so, and the time span of each separation.

May 4th, 2009

Crunch time. Rehearsals start tomorrow morning.

Today, I go to the Dodger's office to get a dramaturgy packet, a script (finally!), a vocal score, dialect recordings, a CD of the Seasons original recordings, a packet with pictures and names of the National Tour cast, a packet with pictures and names of the Toronto cast, and a list of doublings.

Doublings, you ask? Yes! One of the stylistic techniques Frankie Valli used in his original recordings was a doubling of his and other voices. In other words, there was always more than one voice singing each vocal line. While you hear Frankie Valli in the foreground, you also hear another voice (usually Frankie Valli again) in the background singing the exact same thing. *Jersey Boys* mimics this technique by fully utilizing its large cast. According to the score I received today, there are always two people doubling nearly every word I sing. And there are two or three doubling what Frankie sings, two doubling what Nick sings, and two doubling what Bob sings. What an amazing thing! Broadway shows have often used singers in the orchestra pit to augment the sound, but I can't recall a show using live, onstage doubling before. This proves to me that, even in the ensemble tracks, nobody in the cast of *Jersey Boys* has any time to relax.

Returning from the Dodger's office, I highlight my new script, spend a few hours learning another scene, and have a wonderfully theatrical talk with my wife. "You are always talking about the Dodgers these days," she says.

"Well, the Dodgers will be paying our rent for the next year."

"Oh, I know," she continues, "I just find it funny that we always refer to theatre producers as the somethings. The Dodgers. The Shuberts. The Nederlanders. I am pretty sure that the actual Shuberts aren't there anymore; and were there even any actual Dodgers?"

"Don't think so."

"And yet we name them as if they are a family of people with the same last name running this large, theatrical business."

"It's a tradition, I guess. Like the Ringling brothers."

I have no better answer than that. And I'm pretty sure Mr. Ringling and his brother (the other Mr. Ringling) aren't still running the circus.

ACT II

REHEARSING IN NEW YORK

SCENTED CANDLES, JERSEY ACCENTS, & MASHED POTATOES

May 5th, 2009

Today is the first day of the rest of my life. (Or at least the next big chunk of my life.) I have my first rehearsals, in various locations, from 10:00 a.m. to 6:00 p.m. I rise very early to work on memorizing lines; I am almost to the end of the script with a first pass at knowing them. Then I have too much coffee, and pack. I throw a couple bottles of water into my backpack, along with my digital recorder, pencils, script, blank note paper, and my daily planner.

My first call is at the Upper West Side apartment of Adam Ben-David, conductor of the Broadway Company of *Jersey Boys*. He is well known for his work on rock musicals, and his job is to teach me the entire score in three hours. I can't sight read music. I have to record somebody playing it for me, and then sing along with the recording until the parts become ingrained in my head. Due to this lack of ability, I am forever intimidated by conductors.

I arrive at his apartment ten minutes early so I will be ready to begin exactly at 10:00. I am greeted by the smell of scented candles and a furry little dog. I am very allergic to scented candles. And dogs. Awesome.

Adam is very cool to be around. He's a fast talker, and he keeps answering his phone to get updates on the Tony Award nominations that are being announced today in Midtown. He takes a call, laughs and talks and drops a thousand theatrical names, then comes right back to the piano. Even with these fun interruptions, we manage to get through the entire score, getting every note into my digital recorder.

And there are a lot of notes. I sing in twenty songs, and each of them has pretty complex harmonies. Ron Melrose created these arrangements, and I know now that he left no rhythm, note, or phrasing untouched. When we finish the last song, Adam says something completely bizarre to me. He is possibly being sarcastic, but I don't think so. I think these musical directors just have a different sense of how actors learn their music. Adam says, "Well, that's it. We're finished. There is so little music in this show; it's easy, right?" (Ya…right.)

After a lunch break, which isn't really a break since I spent it traveling to the Dodger's rehearsal space in Midtown, I meet my own personal director, Shelley Butler. *Jersey Boys* is so big worldwide, and Des McAnuff is now busy running the Stratford Festival in Canada, that there are a few other directors that were hired to rehearse new people like me. These associates and assistants have memorized what Des says about every moment in the show, and it is their job to first impart that knowledge to me, and then exert their own creativity in helping me find the way to something truthful. So, they have a tricky job. They are recreating someone else's work, but they have to have enough of their own smarts to make that work look good on me. Good luck, Shelley!

We begin with introductions. We'll be spending a ton of time together over the next two months and we need to establish a basic working relationship. Shelley will be rehearsing me here in New York, and then will re-join me in Toronto in a few weeks, staying there through my opening. Her husband is West Hyler, who is the associate director of *Jersey Boys* and Des McAnuff's right-hand man. West isn't available to rehearse me because he is mounting the Australian premier of the show as we speak. Currently, I am the second Tommy that Shelley will be putting in to *Jersey Boys*. She's really nice, humble, and very interested in finding my version of this character, as she knows the super bad-ass thing isn't really me. (Nice. Three minutes in and she already knows I am not a super bad-ass.)

We spend four hours doing table work, and I feel really in my element. Table work encompasses all the preliminary talks that actors and directors have to have before actually getting up and staging anything. The table work can be about getting to know the dramaturgy of the play, deciding on motivations for actions, discussing character relationships, or just about anything else pertinent to how the show will play out. I know most of my lines as we work through the scenes, and feel proud to show her this! (This is dumb. I know.) And I learn a whole lot more about Tommy DeVito. What a guy he was. And is. He was actually in jail for a while in the 70s. That's after having numerous Top Ten hits and selling millions of records, and was while "December, 1963 (Oh, What A Night)" was on the charts. He still lives in Las Vegas. Bad-ass. I should drop him an email someday.

Now I have to stop writing and go work on the harmonies I learned today. I am exhausted and all I want to do is go to bed, but I have to get cracking. Rehearsal never ends when I get home; it only ends when I can't keep my eyes open any longer. Maybe I'll just work on the music while sitting in bed with Cara. She curled up on the couch with me as soon as I arrived home tonight, asking me all kinds of questions about my day. It's nice to be with someone who (1) understands the business, and (2) knows how hard I worked to get here.

May 6th, 2009

Today begins really early because Meg asks me to stop by her office to go through the contracts and riders she just received from the Canadian producers. I thought this would be a quick meeting, but it ends up taking an hour to get through the legal paperwork associated with working in another country, and the many and varied clauses associated with doing this particular show. For example, I am not allowed to perform any songs that are in the show in any public place while I am under contract. No "Can't Take My Eyes Off Of You" at a wedding or cabaret—that's in writing.

And here's a crazy thing: about halfway through our meeting, Meg and I realize that my contract with her expired six months ago. Neither of us had noticed the lapse until now.

"So, Meg, would you like to re-sign me?"

"Yes, Dan. Would you like to be re-signed?"

"Well... Let me consider..."

"Dan."

"Yes?"

"Dan."

"Yes, Meg. Of course, Meg. Anything you say, Meg. You helped get me this far, Meg!" She isn't into my little jokes, I think.

The first part of my rehearsal day was to be, according to the schedule, two hours of "scene work" with Shelley. In reality, we don't really work on the scenes; we just lay out a lot of blocking. "Blocking" is an old theatrical term for the exact movements an actor makes on stage. This being a musical, all of the blocking is done in relation to numbers that are painted on the front edge of the stage floor. For instance, I am to say this line while walking stage left to number six, then speak the next one while walking three steps downstage and right to number two. Very precise. Shelley has a script with all of this information in it, and it is a very thick script.

After that blocking session, I have a two-hour meeting with the dialect coach, Stephen Gabis. What a neat guy! Stephen works with all the *Jersey Boys* companies throughout the world, and has done extensive research on this particular version of the mid-New Jersey dialect. He loves to tell stories, and launches into fifteen different accents while telling them. His first story today lasts a full twenty minutes, and my recorder is running the entire time.

I feel pretty good about my basic Jersey accent, but he helps me refine it to a truer time period. The specific accent for Tommy DeVito is one born of an Italian family that moved from the boroughs of New York City into the small cities of New Jersey. I would consider it more a New York accent than a Jersey accent, but Stephen tells me it is a New Jersey regionalism that isn't really heard at all today. There are rules to follow, rules like dropping the final "r" sound in a word, but only if the next word in the sentence begins with a consonant. However, if a word begins with a vowel, you vocalize the "r" sound. This is great stuff.

To further prove how the *Jersey Boys* franchise has gone global, but remains grounded in the Tri-State area, Stephen is going to have a dialect session with the Australian Frankie Valli via Skype, as soon as he finishes with me. It is 7:00 a.m. down under, so I imagine the actor is going to appear in his bathrobe.

When Stephen's Skype session begins (on a giant, flat-screen monitor in the Dodger's conference room), I go down the hall to my first choreography session. Caitlin Carter is my own personal choreographer, and she scares me. She's nice! Very, very nice! But scary. She is fast and fierce and wants to barrel through these moves at a quicker rate than I am ready for. (She doesn't know how long it took me to learn that stuff on YouTube.) She wants the moves close to perfect right away, and she doesn't pause very often to give me time to write stuff down. Just like I need to record my harmony lines so I can reference them later, so too do I have to write down every move of choreography so that I can remember the details when practicing back at my apartment. I don't learn the moves by doing them a few times in the rehearsal studio; I learn the moves by reviewing them a hundred times in my bedroom.

"Caitlin, you do know I'm not really a dancer, right?"

"But you've had dance classes?"

"Well, sure, but..."

"And you're a musical theatre actor, right?"

"Yeah, of course, but..."

"And you're playing a lead in *Jersey Boys*, right?"

"I sure am, but..."

"So, you're a dancer. Stop talking and repeat what I do."

We begin with "I Go Ape." This is a very quick bit in the show, with very minimal choreography. Caitlin teaches it fast, lets me run through it a few times with her, then stands back to watch me do it by myself. The choreography amounts to eight counts of eight, and I think I mess up five of them. My feet go the wrong way, my guitar neck goes up instead of down, my butt doesn't shimmy hard enough (it can shimmy more?). All in all, I am no good. But, rather than fix things right there, Caitlin decides to leave me with my notes and move on to another song.

She tells me we'll start learning the Big Three. The Big Three is a climactic section of the first act that includes the Four Seasons' first three No. 1 hits performed back-to-back with hardly a break in between: "Sherry," "Big Girls Don't Cry," and "Walk Like A Man." The choreography for "Sherry" is divided into two parts: Sherry One and Sherry Two. Sherry One is pretty simple to do (just a lot of shuffles back and forth), but looks incredible onstage because live video cameras show the guys as if they were on *American Bandstand*. Sherry Two comes across as more presentational because it moves to the front of the stage as if the Seasons are giving a concert, but still pretty easy to do. What is not easy to do, however, is memorize these moves when I don't know yet exactly what I will be singing. In other words, I am taught these moves as they correlate to the main lyric of the song, but Tommy DeVito does not sing the main lyric of the song, he sings backups and echoes and repeats. So, I know that a big task in front of me will be to figure out where these moves fall with the words I will actually have to sing. Work to be done on my own, I guess. Work I should probably be doing right now instead of writing this entry.

We finish "Sherry" in a couple hours and move on to "Big Girls Don't Cry." I like the beginning of this song because, for just a little bit, I can actually just stand there and play the song on the guitar. While I don't know yet exactly what I will be playing live and what I will be faking, it seems clear to me already that some of these songs have far too much dancing around to be able to play well on guitar! But at least "Big Girls" seems possible. For now.

I feel pretty good about my learning curve with this song, for I am picking up the slick moves fairly quickly. I am frustrated, then, when we get to this part in the middle where I am supposed to do a little solo dance bit. I am supposed to look cool. I am supposed to look like a rock star having a bit of fun. But I do not look cool. And I do not look at all like I am having fun. The dance solo is a variation on the Mashed Potato, and it just does not look good on me. Caitlin says that I may be able to do a different dance solo instead, but that I should work on this one first, to see if I can get it. And when we move on, as if to pour salt on my wound, I realize that I have to do this little solo twice in the song. More homework.

May 7th, 2009

Today begins with four hours of table work with Shelley. We really should be doing a blocking rehearsal, but the studio is being used for another project. Shelley compliments me, "You are really picking up on the beats of these scenes. And you seem to be getting the overall character of Tommy. I'm impressed at how quickly it is happening."

I would like to take credit for this, but the truth is I have been studying a bootleg of Christian Hoff's performance. (Anything is available on the internet these days.) While I can't possibly copy him directly, because we are very different people, I find it extremely helpful to see where the rhythms of the scenes and speeches should be. *Jersey Boys* is tightly scored, and too much rhythm differential would cause the underscoring to either run out or finish too early. I won't ever tell Shelley this, but so far I am just copying Christian's rhythms until I figure it all out for myself.

After a lunch break, I am asked to carry the practice guitar ten blocks to my next rehearsal location. It is held at Ripley-Grier Studios on the 16th floor of an office building on 8th Avenue; I am very, very familiar with this location. I audition at Ripley-Grier at least a few times a week, waiting for hours in its hallways. I have rehearsed three shows here. A popular place, it is filled with actors of every level, making it very fun to people-watch. It's painted with a kind of tropical theme. And it has its own cool little coffee shop. But the greatest part? The sign on my studio says *"Jersey Boys,"* and that makes me the one who people are poking their heads around to look at. Any rehearsal is fun to peek at, but a rehearsal for a mega-show like *Jersey Boys* makes me quite the spectacle! I make three unnecessary trips to the bathroom just so I can be seen coming in and out of the rehearsal room door.

Caitlin and I spend three hours learning more choreography and cleaning that which I already learned. "Walk Like A Man" has less foot work than the previous two numbers, and I am really much better with less foot work. I don't feel like an idiot doing this number, so Caitlin suggests we run the Big Three back-to-back like it plays in the show. And then I feel like an idiot.

I mess up about ten times in this first run-through, but it is all right because we just run it all again. And again. And again. My mistakes are fewer as time goes by, but I am so worn out that I can't think straight. Or stand straight.

What a workout it is! I am going to sweat my balls off in this show. Please pardon my phrasing, but I swear that is exactly what is going to happen.

"Terrific job today," Caitlin tells me at the end of the night. "You feeling ok?"

"I feel great, Caitlin. This is totally fun."

"Good. It should be. Hey, Dan?"

"Yeah, Caitlin?"

"You are really, really sweaty."

Jeff Madden, Quinn VanAntwerp, Daniel Robert Sullivan, Michael Lomenda
©Joan Marcus

I go home, clean up, and now am sitting up in bed with Cara asleep beside me. Again. She has left a Post-it note on her forehead: "Up early. Had to go to bed. Love u." I cannot go to sleep yet because I have to work on my harmonies. But I keep looking down at Cara and can't help feeling sad. I know she will most likely be with me all summer, but I am looking down the pike at a year of uncertainty with our schedules. No matter how it works out, I know I will not be sleeping beside her at the end of every day. The hardest thing about working in the theatre is leaving. Theatre work is always about goodbyes.

May 8th, 2009

Tomorrow I leave for Toronto, so today I spend two hours on the phone with Verizon working out a Canadian cell phone plan. To choose the best balance of minutes and cost, one needs a top-secret algorithm and degrees in quantum chaos and equidistribution number theory. I have none of these things, so I choose the plan that's on sale.

Because of my long conversation about cell phone plans, I do not have time to review the Big Three choreography this morning. So, when I arrive for my three hours of dance rehearsal and we jump right into a run-through of everything I have learned so far, I am struggling. I should have done better.

We move on to learn "Dawn." This song, too, is divided into sections: Dawn One, Dawn Two, and Dawn Three. Dawn One is in front of live cameras, just like Sherry One. It is a nice little bit of choreography with some slides that look like Flamenco dancing. The trickiest part of this section will be getting the angle of my guitar to match the angle of Nick's bass exactly, but I can't really get this specific until I rehearse with the guy playing Nick. Oh, and the other tricky thing is that the darn Mashed Potato makes an appearance in this song too. I am starting to really dislike Mashed Potatoes. Dawn Two moves into a live concert scenario, just like Sherry Two. The choreography is also pretty easy, but also extremely specific with its angles. This time, it is not just the angle of my guitar that matters, but the angle of my body relative to my microphone. Caitlin jumps all over me about this, but honestly I can hardly tell the difference between being at a 45° angle to the microphone and being at 70°. (I'm positive one needs a special mathematics degree for this too.) By the time I run these two parts of "Dawn," our rehearsal is over and it is time for me to clean the sweat off myself, change out of my disgusting tee-shirt, and go into blocking rehearsal with Shelley.

Shelley and I get a lot done in our four hours of blocking. I now know, and have rehearsed, all the blocking for Act One. Quite the accomplishment based on how precise all that blocking is. And because I pretty much know all of my lines, I am able to actually run the act, minus the songs. It is fun. There are construction workers outside the studio window and I think they are really enjoying my performance. It is weird, of course, not having any other actors to work with, but at least Tommy spends much of the first act just talking to the audience (so I talk to the Ironworkers of Local 361). On that note, I've just realized how much of a difference it is to rehearse a show without any other actors. I am learning the show very precisely, but I am not

73

really "feeling" it at all yet because there is no give and take. I don't want to sound pretentious here, but it is almost like the art has been taken out. No, that's not right. Rather, it is like the art hasn't been inserted yet.

Caitlin remains at the studio for much of my blocking rehearsal, I think because she has some business in the office. She comes back to visit during one of my breaks and the three of us get into a conversation through which I learn a few interesting tidbits. First, they tell me that Sergio, the choreographer, is much more active in casting *Jersey Boys* companies now than when the show was first mounted; so the crop of guys are usually better dancers than originally intended. (Me too? Nah, probably not.) Second, they tell me that the Broadway Company actually has less choreography in it because Sergio has added sections of dance as additional productions have been mounted. Third, Jeremy Kushnier is one of the favorites, and his movement should be used as a model. (Um, yeah. Ok. I won't be able to do the Mashed Potato the way I imagine he does it. Ever.)

Late today, I find out about a small financial bonus. My agent calls to remind me that she only gets 5% of my salary while I am in rehearsal, as opposed to the 10% she will receive for the rest of my contract. This may not seem like a lot, but it adds a nice pile of money to our very tight budget. Rehearsal salary is much less than what my performance salary will be, and we are trying to create a budget that allows Cara to be with me all summer and not have to worry about making money. She is not allowed to work in Canada, after all.

Oh, man. I'm going to Canada tomorrow.

REHEARSING IN TORONTO

SKYLINES, BANNERS, & SLICK MOVES

May 9th, 2009

Here we go.

I fly to Toronto early in the morning. After leaving Cara to catch my train to the airport, I cry. I didn't expect that to happen. I thank her for letting me do this because, let's face it, she is about to endure a lot of separation for the sake of me following my dreams.

I have been to Canada only once before, and that was just a day trip to a small winery on an island in Lake Erie. Toronto is, obviously, a big city. Flying in, I can see the city bunched up near the edge of Lake Ontario and gradually thinning out northward to the horizon. The CN Tower dominates my impression of the skyline. When you look at the skyline of New York, the Empire State Building looms, but doesn't dominate. There is balance to the arc of New York's building tops. But here in Toronto, the CN Tower grabs your eye and doesn't let you see much else.

The company manager and his partner greet me at the airport. They are extremely welcoming as we jump in their car and embark on a quick tour of the city. My first thought is that the city seems very calm; my second thought is that every streetlamp on every main road has a *Jersey Boys* banner on it. I feel famous already! It is Saturday, and I arrive early enough that I will be able to see both the matinee and the evening performances. First though, I am delivered to my hotel and spend a half-hour running choreography in front of my 12th floor window that overlooks the theatre. This is my most exciting rehearsal so far; it is all starting to feel real.

I grab a shower, and then make my way over to the theatre's stage door. From the moment I enter the building, I hear, "Are you the new Tommy?" time and time again. The doorman, the security guard, a stagehand, and a guy holding a case of beer all ask me this question before I even make it down the hallway. I arrive at the stage management office and meet the team, then my new production stage manager, Cindy Toushan, takes me around to meet the cast. One by one faces appear before me, all of them kind…and inquisitive. I have memorized some of the faces from the list of headshots I was given, so I impress a few people when I say, "Oh, you must be _____."

And then I meet Jeremy Kushnier. Now, I'm a theatre geek. I know I am. So meeting this theatrically famous guy would have been a cool thing for me even if I wasn't taking over for him in the biggest blockbuster musical in this entire country. My first impression of Jeremy is that he is very laid back, and this impression would carry through to his choices as Tommy. I tell him I hear he has been sick the past few days.

"Yeah," he says. "Strep throat. I would have been out today, too, but I wanted to be here for you." Cool, Jeremy. Cool.

I then meet what feels like two hundred other people, after which I'm led into the house to take my seat. I get chills when the music starts. It has been more than a year since I've actually seen the show, and it is better than I remember. Unbelievable. Rocking. Bright. Heartfelt. Loud, but intimate. Amazing.

But I've got to get to work.

I am here to get an impression of Jeremy's work and see where I fit in this mold. So, my first impressions of him are that he is slick and very likable. He speaks in a very high voice. He speaks fast, and his movements are small and sharp. Oh boy. This is not quite where I have been finding my Tommy to be. With Shelley's help, my Tommy is becoming a bit brasher, a bit deeper in my voice, and a bit bolder, somewhat like a bull in a china shop. Both interpretations seem legitimate, but now I am thinking that I will have to take on some of Jeremy's qualities just to fit in with the rest of the actors up there.

And you know what else I am reminded of today? This is a big, big, big role. Oh. My. God.

Oh, and you know what else? The guy playing Bob Gaudio is Quinn VanAntwerp, the actor I heard resonate through the walls at one of my auditions at Chelsea Studios so many, many months ago.

REHEARSING IN ORLANDO

UNDERWEAR DANCING, ROBBING BANKS, & SOLITARY RUN-THROUGHS

May 10th, 2009

I rise early, as has become my custom (by necessity, not by choice). I make coffee in my hotel room and work on choreography for two hours in front of the window, this time in my underwear. Cara would kill me if she knew I was doing this. She hates it when I assume that no one can see me. Apparently, dancing in my underwear is a sight for her eyes only, according to our relationship rules. But if any of these Canadians see me today it will be a really funny image for them: a guy with nothing but underwear, a guitar, and wild bed head flailing through his version of the Mashed Potato at 8:00 in the morning.

After my private rehearsal, I go for a short walk around the neighborhood, just to see what it's like. It has a few nice restaurants, a movie theatre, a few coffee shops, a Staples, and a Dairy Queen. And the theatre. And that's it. Nothing else. Ok, I've learned that we are kind of the only game in this part of town.

I want to buy something to take over to the theatre for the cast, so I go to the nearby supermarket and grab a few nice bunches of strawberries and some chocolate. (The fact that these are sexy foods usually reserved for lovers and those staying in a luxury suite at the Hilton doesn't cross my mind.) I learn my first thing about food shopping here in Canada: they don't take American Express! So, I pull out the MasterCard I haven't used in years and hope that it is still active. If it is not active, I am probably going to be in trouble for eating one of the strawberries on my way to the cashier. No problem, though, the card works.

I bring the fruit and a nice card over to the theatre, leaving them in the green room with a note that says I am looking forward to coming back and getting to know everyone better. It feels weird to have met my cast, but not be learning the show with them. If a new quarterback has been signed by the New York Giants, he doesn't go learn the playbook with a bunch of guys in Florida who happen to be running the same forward passes. (Afterthought: That is probably be the only sports metaphor I will ever use in my life. I am amazed I could even remember the name of New York's team. I don't know if the Giants are any good or if they have ever won a World Series...)

I watch the matinee, then jump in a cab that is waiting (yes, waiting) to take me to the airport.

"Are you one of the *Jersey Boys*?' the driver asks.

"Yup."

"Did you just get off the stage?!"

"Yup." I am such a liar. But it feels so good to say.

After a brief layover, my plane arrives in Orlando after midnight. The producers arranged a rental car for me, but sadly it is at a place that closed at midnight. Only one place, Budget Rental, is still open, but since it is just about the end of their day too, they only have one car available. No problem. I am sure I will be reimbursed by *Jersey Boys* for their mistake. While they finish filling out the paperwork, their computer system shuts down automatically because it is past closing time. The employee actually has to call a manager at home to figure out how to get the system back online; needless to say I am very late getting out of there with a car. I have directions, so I begin driving towards Walt Disney World Resort. What I do not have, however, is cash, and the first thing I notice about the highway I get on is that it's a toll road. When I arrive at the tollbooth, I explain that I have just come from Canada, am here on business, and am so sorry but I don't have any money.

Do they have an ATM I can use?

"No," I am told. "You just need to take this paper with you and promise not to make this mistake again."

A promise? That's it? I'm definitely not in New York anymore. The paper, incidentally, is very funny and talks about how understanding the highway commission wants to be to tourists and other visitors. They praise themselves in this paper for allowing the occasional freebie, and I praise them, too.

I praise them even more when I encounter a second tollbooth fifteen miles down the road. Once again, I explain my situation and am given a second, very nice note from the highway commission.

When I finally arrive at the hotel, I actually feel like I am on vacation. There are palm trees galore, signs telling me about breakfast with Mickey, and a gigantic gift shop. I am starving, so I go to the hotel store and buy a sandwich and a beer and bring them both to my room so I can unpack and settle in. I will be here for two weeks, I think (I'm losing track of the days), and I want to feel comfortable.

While eating, I rearrange the furniture to give myself the rehearsal space that I know I will need. Half of the hotel room becomes my stage, clean and empty with plenty of room for Mashed Potatoes. When I finish the new design, I step outside my room onto the shared balcony, just to breathe for a bit. My short meditation is interrupted when the room next to mine opens up and a German man in his underwear asks me, very sternly, if I have been banging on his door.

"Of course I have not been banging on your door," I tell him. But then, five minutes later, a security guard walks up to me and asks the same question. Welcome to Disney World! I assure the security guard that German men in their underwear are not usually my type, and that he probably just heard me rearranging furniture through the very thin walls of this populist resort.

It's 3:30 a.m. and not even an irate German man can keep me from drifting in and out of sleep as I write. I check my email for the rehearsal schedule and discover that I will have only a few hours of rehearsal each day because the people who will be teaching me the show are actually in the National Tour and they open here in two days. Ugh. I need more than a few hours a day of rehearsal to get this stuff right. How am I going to immerse myself in the show if I am only rehearsing a few hours a day? On the other hand, this will give me plenty of time to run things over and over by myself, so at least I will know well the things I learned. I will have no excuse not to know things well. Maybe it's good to have lots of time by myself. I still have more harmonies to learn, after all.

May 11th, 2009

Today is, officially, my only day off for the week. My brain can't afford to actually take the day off, but I at least give my exhausted body what it needs and sleep until 11:30 a.m., and then begin working. I sit with my coffee and work on harmonies. I use the stage I created and the small mirror hanging on the wall to go over the choreography I have learned so far, then decide to go down to the pool to review my lines (I lead a tough life).

When I go outside in the light of day, I realize this resort looks nothing like the pictures I saw online. Though it's nice enough, it is not a fancy resort, and actually seems more like a glorified motel. It does have a hot tub, though, and I sit near it while running my lines. Would you believe it? I know them all. Every one, no mistakes. Ok! I'm getting there.

I find myself needing changes of scenery to keep my brain attentive, so I spend the rest of the day, and long into the night, fluctuating between my in-room rehearsal studio and various locations outside. Inside my room, I review choreography while listening to harmony parts on my digital recorder, putting the two elements together for the first time. (I don't get through any songs without messing up. Yet.) Outside, I wander the paths of the neighborhood listening to harmonies and trying to get through at least a few songs without a vocal mistake. I work from 11:30 a.m. until 2:00 a.m. with only a quick break for a shower and a muffin, and another for a sandwich from the lobby. Some day off!

I shouldn't be sarcastic about that, though. In reality, I spend my day across from Walt Disney World in perfect weather working on the kind of show I have dreamed about being in since I was a little boy. It is amazing when I really stop and think about what I am doing, but it is hard to stop and think about what I am doing when there is just so much of it to do.

Tomorrow, my rehearsal will begin with a choreography session led by the National Tour's dance captain. Now that I have a relationship with Caitlin and know how she likes to work in rehearsal, I am nervous to have to start a relationship with a new dance instructor. Everything makes me nervous these days, doesn't it?

Even my marriage.

"I have been crying for half an hour," Cara says in a late-night call, "How are we going to do this for a year? I have no one to talk to."

"I'm right here, hon. My phone is always on."

"Yes, but it doesn't feel like you are right here when you are down there because down there is very far from right here."

"You sound like Dr. Seuss." (Afterthought: Not a smart thing to say.)

"Huh? Daniel, I don't even understand you."

"I know, I'm sorry. I was making a dumb joke. I'm sorry. You are feeling alone," I say.

"I'm not feeling alone. I am alone."

I've been away from home exactly sixty-seven hours, which is exactly sixty-six hours too long.

May 12th, 2009

Today is a major workday, but also ends up being a day of major excitement and inspiration. I begin by driving ten miles (still in a funk from last night) to a rehearsal studio the producers rented. There are no studios at the theatre *Jersey Boys* is playing in downtown, so they found one a little off the beaten path. I arrive early and observe a stilt-walking team rehearsing jumps and flips. Ok, so they have a cool job, too.

When they finish, I enter the room and begin running through the Big Three while waiting for the dance captain, Kara Tremel, to arrive. In New York, I rehearsed with just Caitlin or Shelley in the room, sometimes with an accompanist on the piano. But here in Florida, the dance captain arrives with the production stage manager, associate musical director, and props master. This is the real deal now, my friends. A lot of money is being spent on me today.

After brief introductions, they want to see what I know. So, the associate musical director plays straight through "I Go Ape," "Sherry," "Big Girls Don't Cry," "Walk Like a Man," and "Dawn" without a break. I sing something close to my vocal parts and dance something close to my choreography. I do not totally rock it, but (all things considered) I do not embarrass myself.

We work for four hours cleaning choreography for the portions I was already taught and learning just two new parts: Dawn Three and "Beggin." Dawn Three is the culminating theatrical moment of Act One, when the performance is turned around backwards so that the audience sees the Four Seasons performing in concert from a reverse perspective. For most of the audience, this is the first time experiencing what it feels like to be on a huge stage and lit by so many bright lights. "Beggin" is a fun number to do, and has a lot of fancy footwork. I am told that the hardest thing in this song will be matching guitar angles with the actor dancing next to me, but for now the hardest thing is just getting my feet to move in the right direction. I write down every little move (Kara lets me have short breaks to do this) so that I can remember it all in my hotel room later.

After rehearsal, I drive over to the nearest gas station for a perfect dinner of coffee and hot dogs. I eat in the car on my way to downtown Orlando, listening to my harmonies the entire way. After taking far too long to find parking, I go into the Bob Carr Performing Arts Centre. This theatre has the biggest auditorium of any legit theatre I've seen. It holds twenty-five hundred people, and feels like it stretches out forever. I am introduced all around.

The *Jersey Boys* performing company is comprised of:

- fourteen regular cast members (six of whom understudy other roles, too),

- an alternate who performs the role of Frankie twice a week,

- three male swings who cover four or five roles apiece (a swing is an understudy who does not perform a regular role each night, but remains at the theatre just in case),

- a female swing who covers all three female roles,

- and ten musicians.

I think I just met all of them tonight. I am given an ID badge that identifies me as a cast member(!), and move out into the house to find an empty seat. There are very few. I meet up with some of the swings out in the house. They are watching the show tonight because this is a very exciting performance for the company. Remember Buck, who I auditioned with so many times back in New York? Well, after a year of being an understudy for Bob and never having the chance to go on, he performs the role for the first time tonight. His wife is watching as well, and can barely control her enthusiasm. I am asked to sit with this contagiously enthusiastic group, and instantly feel like part of the family.

So, what are my first impressions of this cast? Buck is terrific and innocent and sounds strong. He is a much better Bob than I could have been. The show as a whole seems broader, probably because they are playing in a much bigger space than any other company. The jokes all land. The choreography is clean and fierce. And best of all, the Tommy DeVito is different than Jeremy. The actor, Matt Bailey, is terrific and clearly has his own spin on the part. He sings with a fuller voice. He is much more aggressive. And, therefore, he gives me visible permission to find my own take on the character. I know this should be obvious and may seem kind of silly to put into words, but this show is directed with such detail that I was starting to feel like there was only one way to do it, and that I had to find that way. But there's not only one way. This Tommy is entertaining hundreds of thousands of people with a different spin, and I can too. I'm invigorated. I'm ready for more rehearsal where I can play and experiment. I'm also very tired and am going to bed now.

May 13th, 2009

I have four hours of blocking rehearsal onstage today with the production stage manager, Eric Insko. This man knows the show backwards and forwards, and can tell you within inches where anyone should be standing at any given moment. His knowledge of *Jersey Boys* is epic.

This rehearsal is the first time they allow me to actually stand on a *Jersey Boys* set, and it feels wild. Like every set of all the shows I've ever been a part of, it seems a lot smaller when you are on it.

There is a bridge section raised high in the air, and every time I walk across it, I feel like I am going to fall off. There is also a small perch section that I will have to stand on many times. This section rises ten feet above the stage, twenty feet above the front row, and has only a short railing to hold on to. And my big discovery of the day? The floor of that perch is made of Plexiglas, so you see right through it when you stand up there. I go up five times today and still can't get rid of the dizzying feeling.

While working on blocking with Eric, I don't really say my lines full-out. In fact, I realize that I haven't ever said my lines full-out to anyone. I am forever marking my performance because I am forever working on some element that is not character, voice, or intention. In order to really learn about this character, I need to speak and interact. It is hard to get in the head of Tommy and track his thoughts while being taught where to stand and how to dance; and not saying the lines full out doesn't help either. I have always worked best, and learned most, with full run-throughs of scenes.

On the other hand, if I want to say my lines full out then I should say them full out. Maybe the truth is that I am nervous about being judged. I'm embarrassed. A ridiculous reason, but I think it might be true. I have worked for two years for this coveted role, and I am embarrassed to speak the lines aloud because I'm not good enough yet.

I have an hour of rehearsal with the National Tour's musical director. There are a lot of people helping me learn this show, but I am still not sure why I am learning it here in Orlando instead of in Toronto with my actual company. (And I will come to see that I never learn why I rehearsed in Orlando instead of Toronto.)

The musical director and I go through all of my harmonies just to make sure I am singing the correct lines. And I know them all! I am relieved at that. Now, I have to repeat a few of them once or twice to correct myself, but in general the hours I have spent listening to and singing the harmonies have paid off.

When we are finished, he closes his book and says, "Well, you know all your parts." Note that he does not say, "Well, you sound great."

"Yeah, I guess I pretty much know them all," I reply.

"Yes, you do."

The subtext here is that *Jersey Boys* cast members have been fired outright for not singing up to the company's standards. This is a fact. I may know all my parts, but if I don't do them well then I will be fired. That is how this world works. I wanted the musical director to say I sounded great. But he did not.

May 14th, 2009

Rehearsal is scheduled back in the stilt-walker's studio from 2:00-5:00 p.m. today, but at 1:08 I get a call from Kara, the dance captain. "Where are you? Rehearsal was supposed to start at 1:00." Great. Luckily, I am already on my way to the studio, having thought I would arrive a half-hour early. It seems that the rehearsal time changed, and that the change was posted on the callboard at the theatre. But I didn't think to check the callboard at the theatre because I am not in that show! Eric insists he told me about the change, and that may be so. But Eric, I don't deal well with change...

So, my day begins with a negative impression cast upon me, and unfortunately it continues throughout the day. I ask Kara to clarify some of the moves in "Beggin," because I noticed last night at the show that the guys did it slightly different than I do in my room. We check my notes and it turns out that I wrote down the choreography incorrectly. And I practiced a lot. So now I am an expert at the wrong choreography.

We work on "Who Loves You" next. This is a very fun song to do. The number begins with the four guys walking onstage one at a time, building the song verse by verse. As they enter, they look to each other as a way to check in and re-connect. I discover today that every one of these looks is choreographed. Every single one. Walk, walk, snap, snap, look left, step-touch, look right, pivot, snap, snap, look further left. Why do choreographers stage things like walking and looking? Leave that to the individual actor, I say. Of course I haven't staged multiple productions of a Tony Award-winning musical, so I should probably keep my opinions to myself. (Or publish them in a book.) (Hee-hee.)

85

Places, Please!

May 15th, 2009

I have choreography rehearsal onstage for the first time today. This is another expensive rehearsal for the producers, for not only do I have my usual cadre of multiple stage managers, the props master, the dance captain, and the associate musical director, but they need to hire in two local stagehands to move the scenery. Very intimidating.

"You the new guy?" one of the stagehands asks.

"Yeah, I am. I'm Dan; nice to meet you."

"Well thanks, Dan."

"Thanks for what?" I ask.

"The overtime." Then he chuckles.

The work goes well, but I am hesitant to perform full-out in this big, empty space. As these days go by, I am less embarrassed to do a performance full-out and more nervous of getting into habits and choices that don't work. There is still a lot of character-forming to do, and I don't want to get used to doing something any one particular way. Some guys can jump right into a full performance, but I have to step into it gradually. I am forever marking things.

Next, I have a one-hour rehearsal with Ron Melrose, the music supervisor of the show. This is the only hour I will have with him, as he is just in town for a couple days to check in on the tour. This is also the first day I am in front of someone with the power to fire me.

Ron asks whether I have any questions and I say no, why don't we just do it. We sing through the first three songs without stopping, after which he gives me some great notes:

- He says he likes my "bad boy that you want to go home with" quality, that it is similar to Jeremy Kushnier and will be a good swap.

- He says I should accent the consonants in the first song I sing, for it is reassuring for the audience to hear a simple song in English after they have been taken for a ride through the opening number, which is in French.

- He suggests I use a glottal attack every time I say the word, "I" in my first two songs. He says this will accentuate the fact that Tommy is focused on himself.

- He clarifies which speeches are timed out to the underscoring, and emphasizes that I have to finish talking or the song will go on without me.

- And he says there are some songs he would like to hear on my guitar, and others he has deemed too difficult to play smoothly (this is the same conclusion I have drawn). So, while I will play everything live, my guitar amplification will only be turned on during certain songs where I am not moving much and thus can play cleanly. He emails me the guitar charts to work on at my convenience (in other words, every night for the next month).

Ron does not fire me. I love him for that. But he does tell me a great story of an actor who never made it past his callback. In one of the early scenes, the character Hank Majewski gets angry with Tommy, telling him, "Stick to what you know. Rob a bank." This is always a big laugh line. Apparently, an actor auditioning for the role was given this scene to read and thought it was a pretty easy little bit. With frustration, and at the top of his voice, the actor exclaimed, "Stick to what you know, Rob! A bank!" It is amazing what an incorrect pause can do.

May 16th, 2009

Today the cast performs two shows, so my official rehearsal call is only two hours and takes place while the matinee is being performed. Kara and I take over a small portion of the wardrobe room at the theatre. She has me run the numbers in real time just as they are being performed mere yards away, but teaches me the choreography for "Ragdoll" during the few moments between songs. So, my rehearsal is sporadic and disjointed and provides great exercise for my brain.

Kara says I am doing the steps much better now, but that we need to work on my style. Sergio, the choreographer, places big emphasis on the way each character moves, not just what moves he executes. I wonder if this is good? Shouldn't my style just be, well, mine? I guess he is trying to make the movements of each character represent who they are on the inside. I'm sure I will grow to appreciate this, but for now it is just more specifics to work on.

I spend the rest of the day listening to my harmonies while having an Italian dinner, watching the second show from the audience, and rehearsing alone back in my hotel room. Now, in bed, I miss home a lot more than usual. The last show of the season for *Saturday Night Live* is on television right now, and Cara will be attending the wrap party after it is over. I wanted to go to that party with her. Oh, well. Maybe next year.

May 17th, 2009

Another two-show day for the cast means another short rehearsal for me. If I rehearsed only as much as they slot for me to, I would never learn it all!

I am set up in the wardrobe room again. It's funny in there—I have a stage that is marked out by costume racks and three dressing mirrors set up to watch myself. But the costume racks sometimes need to be accessed by the dressers (who chuckle at me), and the mirrors are warped, reflecting only a funhouse version of my sweet, sweet moves.

During my official two-hour call, Kara teaches me the curtain call choreography and helps put some finishing touches on the few gestures I do in my first song, "Silhouettes."

"Dan, I want to tweak your opening number."

"Ok. Cool. What should I do?"

"It is more like what you should not do. I want you to move less. You look cooler if you move less." This cannot possibly be a good thing.

I have now been taught everything in the show, except for three quick bits I have to do with the fight captain. I know my track in *Jersey Boys*. I don't do it well yet, but I officially know everything and that feels pretty good.

Before I go to clean my sweat off and watch the company's two shows, I visit Joseph Siravo in his dressing room. Joseph plays Gyp DeCarlo in the show, and has since the tour was first launched a couple years ago. Joseph is the resident Italian expert (he used to be on *The Sopranos*—what other credentials does he need?) and has offered to go over some pronunciations with me. He is a very nice, very giving man, and boy can he talk! He not only teaches me how to pronounce the Italian words I say in the show, but also about the dialect Tommy's family would have used when speaking Italian, the history of some of the slurred consonant sounds, and the "proper" vowel sounds to watch out for and keep from creeping in. He then promises to email me a five-page document he prepared on the three lines of Italian dialogue in the show. Five pages. For three lines. This guy is very complete.

I watch the first performance of the day standing at the back of the auditorium because every one of those twenty-five hundred seats was sold. For the second show of the day I take control of the wardrobe room, setting up simulations of every prop, guitar, and suit jacket that I will need to run my track in its entirety.

"Ladies and gentlemen, this is your half-hour call. Half-hour until places."

I put on fresh rehearsal clothes and drink some water. I act as if I am going to perform tonight. I want to test myself.

"Ladies and gentlemen, places please. This is your places call."

When the real show begins, I begin too. There is a monitor in the wardrobe room so I can hear every word spoken onstage, but I try to get to the lines a few seconds before Matt Bailey does so I am not relying on him to help me remember. I dance the numbers in real time, speak the words as a few-second preview, and make it through the whole show without a major mistake.

You know what is the greatest thing about this real-time rehearsal? Even though I know the show is fast and furious and I have been sweating through it every day, I realize today that there is some breathing room. I will have moments (if only brief) backstage to grab a drink of water and cool off before launching into the next number. I can do this without passing out. I think.

I decide to go to a party the cast is having tonight. It's a fiesta party, celebrating Cinco de Mayo a couple weeks late. A few of the guys are living in a rented house down the street from the theatre and have decorated it with all kinds of hysterical, Mexican-themed items. Piñatas, giant bowls of nachos, tons of Coronas, and a bathtub made to look like the border between Mexico and the United States (complete with green army men on the US side, and a Barbie doll trying to swim across from the Mexican side). I have a great time, and feel pulled in as a family member once again.

I leave the party pretty early to go back to the hotel and begin my usual routine of working on the show and catching my wife up on the events of the day. When I walk out to the street though, there is a police officer getting ready to ticket every car on the block. The parking regulations on this street are confusing enough that everyone made the same mistake, prompting a neighbor to complain.

"Officer, the owners of these cars are all inside. We're from out of town. We're with *Jersey Boys* down the street." I think this might impress him.

"You're from New Jersey?"

"No. We're with *Jersey Boys*."

"Well wherever you're from, I'm going to ticket these cars if they are not gone in five minutes."

I guess I have encountered the only person in America who has not heard of *Jersey Boys*. But I become a little bit of a party hero when I run back inside and get everybody to move their cars. A cop ruining a great party, it's like college all over again. (Ok, I didn't really go to the type of parties that cops broke up when I was in college, but you get the idea.)

May 18th, 2009

Today is my first wedding anniversary. I celebrate this morning by sleeping in and doing nothing but watching CNN until 2:00 p.m. As much as I love Anderson Cooper, he is not who I would choose to spend my first anniversary with. My first choice is beside me, sort of. You see, last night I had the brilliantly modern idea of leaving the webcam active while Cara and I fell asleep. This meant that, even at 4:00 a.m., I could roll over and see her asleep next to me. Perfect. (Ok, it's also a little freaky. And I snore sometimes, so she probably turned her sound off.)

After much CNN, I rehearse in my room, and all the shuffling back and forth starts wreaking havoc on my left knee (a recurring problem I've had since injuring it in *The Music Man* in college). To help that knee, I decide it is best for the show if I spend an hour soaking in the hotel's hot tub. Yes. I sacrifice my precious time to soak in a hot tub for the sake of the show.

I grab dinner alone at a pub over in Downtown Disney, the families there reminding me a bit too much of the one I have hanging out back in New York. I'm lucky, but lonely. Happy anniversary, honey.

May 19th, 2009

Eric calls a full understudy rehearsal today, so I am able to interact with other actors for the first time. I have worked on this show for two weeks, and never have I spoken the words directly to another human being. Until today.

We begin steadily. Opening speeches. First few songs. Because much of the first section is a direct address to the audience, there is not much difference yet in having the other actors around me. The show moves briskly, the other guys hand my guitars to me at the appropriate times, and the short sections of choreography look pretty cool with all of us doing it together. Then, when we reach the section of "Cry For Me" where The Four Seasons start singing together for the first time, my heart stops. Four guys and four distinct voices. Close harmony. This is the sound of *Jersey Boys*, and there is nothing like this sound.

I am blown away and feel ready to burst from pure excitement. With the mood this song puts me in, the rest of the first act is a blast. "Sherry" has a great harmony that explodes from the first word of the song. "Big Girls Don't Cry" looks great because my movements match up with many of Nick's. "Walk Like A Man" is overpowering as it ends with strong gestures and all of us singing at the top of our lungs.

The Sit-Down scene in Act Two shows Tommy getting kicked out of the group. All the emotions and personalities of the four guys come crashing together. The scene is all about being in the moment and, for my character, really feeling like there is little left to do but kick and scream. It's an intense scene, and it feels absolutely brilliant being able to do it with guys who are equally committed to playing it with full emotion.

During the evening's performance, I run through the show on my own in my cubbyhole in the wardrobe room. It seems to be the standard that a replacement actor spends most of his time rehearsing alone. While a newly mounted show has the luxury of full-length rehearsal days, a show that is already running can only afford to give up its actors a handful of hours each week to rehearse with somebody new. Why? First, performing is exhausting and obviously takes priority. Second, overtime charges kick in pretty early and can run up a large bill for the producer. Thus, I am left to fend for myself.

I poke my head into the hair room on my way out tonight. Because of Cara's work, I have always felt comfortable in hair rooms. It is nice to talk to the three women in there because it makes me feel just a little closer to home.

May 20th, 2009

The understudies join me in the stilt-walker's rehearsal studio again. I feel like I am getting to know these guys, both on and off stage, and we've actually started to build character relationships. Nobody, including myself, is doing anything halfheartedly. But every time I think of how well the interactions are going, I have to remind myself that these are not the actors I will be doing the show with, and that things will be different in just a couple of weeks. Even though *Jersey Boys* is directed within an inch of its life, there are general character relationships that are figured out based on the people actually doing the roles. I have to bully Frankie, for example, but I'm going to bully a small, young Frankie in a very different way than I'm going to bully a slightly taller, solid Frankie. Same thing with Nick. The Tommy-Nick relationship in the show can be more subtle or more combative, depending on who plays each part. Some figuring out needs to be done when I get to Toronto.

I also have a phone meeting with the *Jersey Boys* marketing department today. They want me to approve my press release. Oh, man. I'm going to have a press release.

May 21st, 2009

Another two-show day for the cast and no rehearsal for me. I'm on my own again. Usually their two-show days mean two hours of rehearsal for me, but maybe Eric doesn't want to overwork Kara today. I seem to be a second full-time job for her lately.

Kara's regular dance captain duties include: learning all the choreography and musical staging for every part of the show, watching the show a few times each week to give actors notes on adjustments that need to be made to keep up the choreographer's original intent, leading brush-up rehearsals when necessary, and teaching (sometimes even auditioning) new performers. And on top of this, she is a swing and must be ready to perform any of the three female roles at a moment's notice. So having a day off from me gives her time to check up on everyone else.

My wife finally figures out travel plans for her and the kids today. All in all, the plans make me happy as she and Rachel will be in Toronto with me for much of the summer. Mark will be working at a summer camp this year, so he will only be in Toronto for a little bit, but at least he'll be able to see the show.

Here's how it is shaking down: Cara and Rachel will come up for my opening night, stay a few days, and return to New York. A few days later, when school is over, they will return to Toronto with Mark, who will stay for four days. Then Mark will go to work at the camp, and Cara and Rachel will stay for another two weeks. Cara and Rachel will return to New York for a few days for a previously-planned visit from Rachel's Dad, and then come back to Toronto for the rest of the summer. Such is our hectic life.

May 22nd, 2009

Eric calls my biggest rehearsal yet—seven actors and a full backstage team to give me an onstage run-through of the entire show with all the props and set pieces. I manage to get through the choreography with some sense of style and my lines came to me without -um-er-um-stumbling. I hit all my marks, even though the stage is absolutely littered with colored spike-tape and I have often had a hard time figuring out which marks are the ones I am supposed to be hitting. Pushing the Penthouse Scene bench (we call it the "whore bench" because of the characters that sit on it, not because the bench itself is frisky) and moving the Car Scene seat onto their correct marks will take more practice.

I go to dinner with some of the guys afterwards as a kind of personal celebration. The theatre business, while global and full of newly-graduated faces every year, often feels like a small world. I get to know John Gardiner, the actor who plays Knuckles (and is in the midst of learning to understudy Tommy), and discover a few amazing coincidences that prove to me that we should be friends:

- He is also a good friend of one of my Roundabout Theatre colleagues back in New York.

- We worked for the same theatre playing the same role back in 1998, only missing meeting each other by a few weeks.

- We have the same agent, Meg.

This kind of thing always happens. It is impossible to do a show where you have no connection to at least a few of the people in it. The theatre world may be large, but the pool of people actually working in it is quite small. How small? According to the latest analysis by Actors' Equity Association, only 41.4% of its members worked in the theatre business last year. (That's about 17,000 actors and stage managers out of a membership of about 42,000.) But here's the kicker: those working professionals only found an average of 17 weeks of employment for the whole year. And the median yearly income earned by these workers from theatre jobs was $7,475. The *Jersey Boys* family is not only lucky to be in a great show, but lucky just to have a job.

For the cast's performance this evening, I opt to trail Matt Bailey backstage as he performs his Tommy. I know there is a lot of backstage traffic, and I finally feel ready to learn it. I learn that there are a couple quick-changes. The first quick-change is going into "I'm In The Mood For Love" and has two dressers going to town on Tommy, literally ripping his clothes off down to his underwear and holding up new clothes to dive into. There is no modesty here. The second quick-change is going into "Sherry," and it is then that Velcro shirts come in handy. Tommy has to rip off his first shirt so a dresser can help him into his new one (with a tie). But the new shirt and tie are set up with Velcro, so the dresser just closes it all up, holds out the snazzy red suit jacket, and pushes Tommy towards his waiting guitar. Slick.

I also learn how busy the ensemble is backstage during the show. I've already written about how most of the vocal lines are doubled to create the signature Four Seasons sound, but what I didn't know until tonight is that the cast members doing the doubling are often in the middle of their own quick-changes while singing. (And that much of the Frankie Valli doubling is done by women. What does that say about the range of his voice?!) There is never a break for this ensemble, and no one has time to go back to their dressing rooms to change clothes; all of the costume changes are done in the wings.

Intermission is a different story. During intermission, the actors have about fifteen minutes of free time, and it is spent in a few interesting ways. There are a couple guys who go right for the stereotype and are making their way through *The Sopranos* on DVD. There are a couple who disappear into an upstairs room to work on tap routines (wisely, they rehearse), there are a couple who always seem to have a newly-purchased guitar to play with (wisely, they fine-tune their skills), and there are a few who sit alone in their dressing rooms with music playing (wisely, they steer clear of human contact in an attempt to avoid getting sick of seeing the same people every day).

May 23rd, 2009

I was too tired and talked to Cara for too long to run the show last night, so my morning here in Orlando begins with a full run-through in my room; taking breaks only to sip on coffee.

I drive downtown for the last time to join the company for their final two shows of the week. During the first show, Kara watches me do a wardrobe room run in real time. She has a page or so of notes, but they are all very specific things; there is nothing like, "Hey, you just suck at this number and we need to change everything for you." Actually, she says she can't believe how much better I am doing, but this just makes me wonder how low I set the bar on my first day.

95

During dinner break, I compose a nice note for the cast thanking them for their help. If it weren't for me being here, many of these folks would have had a lot more free time to explore Orlando. (They could have gone to the Holy Land Experience right down the road and had their picture taken with Jesus.) They worked overtime hours for two weeks just because some guy is joining the Toronto cast, and none of them ever complained. There is a supportive atmosphere here and I love being a part of it. I am very grateful for these people. However, this was a lonely time, and I am very happy to be leaving for New York tomorrow.

Before the next show begins, I join some of the boys in the parking lot behind the theatre to toss a football around. I am not good at tossing a football, but I really want to feel like a part of the group, so I jump in…and promptly throw the ball high into a tree. I leave the game (shamefacedly) to say goodbye to everyone individually before the show begins.

"Dan, I really wish you were staying."

"Dan, I can't wait to see you in the role and it would be cool to have you stick around here longer."

"Dan, stop taking jobs from the Canadians."

The comments are nice to hear, and I hope to have made as positive an impression on them as they have made on me. I really like being a part of this global family.

I decide to do something very different and watch this last show from the front row. The volume and intensity of being that close makes me feel giddy all over again. The excitement I feel rehearsing for the show comes and goes in waves, for sometimes it just feels like a whole lot of work. But when some of the work is behind me, like tonight, then the thrill kicks in and I can't wait to perform this thing myself.

After returning to the hotel, packing my things up, and rearranging the room back to its original state, I am ready for dinner. It is 1:30 a.m. I walk a few blocks to Downtown Disney looking for a place to eat, but nothing appears to be open at this hour. I am getting hungrier and hungrier and would be happy eating just chips from a gas station if I could find one. But I can't find one! So after an hour of wandering I come back to the hotel…and discover fresh, hot pizza being served in the lobby.

REHEARSING IN NEW YORK (AGAIN)

NAKED ROOMS, BLONDS, & UNFIT FITTINGS

May 24th, 2009

After a morning driving by those very nice tollbooth operators (with cash in hand this time), I make it back to the Orlando airport. I am sporting new *Jersey Boys* luggage tags; the first of many *Jersey Boys* items I hope to own. I always dreamed of owning one of those awful looking leather jackets with a Broadway show logo on the back. This type of jacket was the signature of a Broadway performer in the 90s, and I want one. But luggage tags are a start, and I silently thank the company manager for giving them to me when the airline attendant checking me in says, "Oh! Are you with *Jersey Boys*?"

"Yes," I say proudly, "I am."

I hope this happens many more times.

I arrive at LaGuardia, get my bags and guitar, and sprint to the nearest cab. I am ready to see my lady! Now, my lady will tell you that I never take cabs because they are expensive and we are perpetually on a tight budget. But this one is reimbursable by the producers, so away I go.

I know I haven't actually been away too long yet, but it feels lengthy because we are looking ahead to an uncertain time. My contract is for at least a year in Toronto, and Cara will be there full time for only two months. I don't know how we are going to manage the year yet, so this two-week absence feels like just one of many, many more to come.

"I missed you."

"I missed you, too."

And I hold her. For a long time.

I unpack quickly, mostly just throwing my clothes into the laundry basket. After unpacking, we go for lunch at Blockhead's, our favorite little

Mexican place, and do a lot of staring. We've been talking twenty times a day so there are no new stories to tell, but right now all we need is to look across the table at each other.

Then we meet Mark in Central Park and toss the football around. I am a little better with the football this time. It doesn't land in any trees.

As we are walking home, Cara and I get into a very serious conversation about communication. Constant communication is the only thing that is going to get us comfortably through this next year (possibly more). And we realize something fun: we have not gone a day without talking to each other since the first moment we met. Not one day.

May 25th, 2009

It was incredibly relaxing to wake up in my own bed this morning. Sleeping next to my beautiful wife was, in a word, satisfying. In another word, completing. In three words, really freakin' sexy.

This is my week off from rehearsal, and it feels strange. I am not on salary this week, for one contract (American) has ended and another contract (Canadian) has yet to begin. But I am now an official member of Canadian Actors' Equity Association, and that feels pretty good. I've always been somewhat active in the American union, serving on multiple committees and contract negotiation teams, so it is neat to be part of a sister organization.

And thanks to the union(s), the three costume fittings I have this week will actually be paid days of work. So, my week off will still have a little money coming in.

Cara comes with me to the fitting today, my first at a new shop that makes just one type of shirt for *Jersey Boys*—the bowling shirts. That's it. And this shop is so incredibly grateful for the work.

Imagine that! They only make one type of costume for the show, but treat the job as if it were a gift. That just goes to show how much of a big business *Jersey Boys* is. The same equation I used with St. Laurie Merchant Tailors can be used here: four guys wear the shirts, plus their two understudies, plus the second Frankie, multiplied by seven companies worldwide, plus replacements that go into the show every year. This is big business for a small costume shop.

And the lady fitting me into a mock-up of the shirt enlightens me about something. "We're lucky," she tells me. "Most of the big shows that are mounted in different countries like Canada and the UK use shops in those countries to build the costumes. But *Jersey Boys* wanted a perfectly uniform look, so they negotiated early on that all companies everywhere would have their costumes built by a few New York shops. It gives them consistency, and it gives us a lot of work."

No wonder this lady is so grateful. She says that costume shops have been hurting for work as Broadway budgets get smaller, and that some of the shops I'll be visiting might have been forced to close their doors had it not been for the popularity of *Jersey Boys*.

I spend the early part of the evening running through the entire show in an empty room in our apartment building. Ordinarily this room is used for exercise classes, but it is empty and available for my use tonight. But because it is not totally private I fear that somebody will walk in on me while I am doing the "Walk Like A Man" sways. That would not be cool. Unless the person walking in is an actor who knows the show. Then it would be the absolute coolest thing ever. (Sadly, none come in. Though I'm not the kind of guy to show off anyway...)

May 26th, 2009

Today is the first day since mid-April that I am not doing a single thing related to *Jersey Boys*, so maybe I shouldn't even be writing. But it is such a great day that I think I'm going to include it anyway.

Today is our first wedding anniversary! Sort of. If you have been reading this closely, you know that our real first wedding anniversary was May 18th, but Cara and I decided long ago to celebrate today, the only day we both have off from work.

We head out to Flushing, Queens early in the morning to one of the most unusual and awesome places I have ever experienced in New York: Spa Castle. It is an adventure to get there, for we have to take the subway out to the end of the line, then run up a hill to catch the shuttle van, and then ride in the cramped backseat ten miles to the location. But it is well worth it.

Spa Castle is billed as a combination of "traditional Asian saunas and luxurious European spas," and has five gigantic floors of self-service bliss. We spend the day in rooftop hot tubs with jets that point every which way (oh yes, every which way), saunas of varying hot temperatures and scents, an ice sauna that we can't last more than a few seconds in, massage chairs, and a naked room.

Wait. Did I just say naked room? Yes, I did. Most of this place is co-ed, but one floor is separated between males and females and is full of giant scented hot tubs where clothing is not permitted.

For an extra charge, we have extreme massages. I call them "extreme" because I am literally picked up and slammed down onto the massage table multiple times. And I like it.

We come back into Manhattan for a fancy dinner on Park Avenue and after eating so much that I feel hatred for my belt, jump in a cab to take us to Midtown. I have a surprise for Cara. For a few years now she has wanted to see *Avenue Q*. I know it is leaving Broadway soon, so I have bought us some great seats. We see the show, laugh like *Lion King* hyenas, and comment how much we love the work the lead actor is doing. That lead actor is Howie Michael Smith, who auditioned with me for *Jersey Boys* way back at the beginning of my journey.

May 27th, 2009

Cara left for Cincinnati this morning. It was a trip planned long before I was offered the out-of-town job, long before we knew this will be my last week in New York for at least a year. I won't see her again for three weeks when we'll meet in Toronto for my opening night. By now, I think anyone reading this knows how I am feeling today.

My own workday begins with an early fitting at yet another costume shop. This shop is the exclusive builder of the "Four Lovers" jacket worn by four guys in the show for just one very short scene.

Then, for a great mini-climax in my rehearsal process, I go to see a matinee of the *Jersey Boys* Broadway Company. I am permitted to sit on the stairs at the side of the auditorium and see the show for free. An usher asks me, "Are you an actor?"

"Yes, I am," and I'm glad to be answering this question.

"Are you going into this show somewhere?"

"Yes, I am," and I'm proud to be answering this question.

"What role will you be playing?"

"Tommy," and I'm bragging with this answer, maybe just a bit.

"Tommy? But you're blond!"

Why is this such an issue?

The stairs I sit on are comfy enough and have a great view of the audience and their reactions. And the reactions to this performance, especially happening so close to New Jersey, are rowdy! But here's the thing: now that I know the show so well, I am much less intimidated by it. No longer does this show seem unattainable or impossible to perform.

And now I see another variation of the Tommy character. This is the fourth version I've seen, and the toughest. Dominic Nolfi is spectacular, and has been playing Tommy for about a year since Christian Hoff left. Dominic has been with *Jersey Boys* since it began out at La Jolla Playhouse in California, and is the only guy I have heard of to understudy both Frankie and Tommy. Imagine the vocal range he must have! And his performances understudying Tommy must have been good, for he was the one chosen to replace the Tony Award-winning performer.

I would not be very effective playing Tommy as tough as I saw him today. I need to play up the small bits of intelligence Tommy shows in the beginning of the show. I need to play up the jokester, the hothead. If Dominic's interpretation of Tommy could easily beat up the other guys, my version of Tommy just thinks he can! I am learning a lot watching these interpretations and am lucky to have all these options to draw from.

101

May 28th, 2009

The alarm is set for very early this morning so I can have a full day of working on the show. Because I only watched the show yesterday instead of running it myself, I was feeling guilty last night and thought I should atone. For me, waking up early when I don't absolutely have to is extreme atonement.

Upon waking, I instantly begin running all of the choreography with my headphones on…in my underwear. Again. Dancing in my underwear is becoming like a fetish. I am in my bedroom, but this time the shades are drawn tightly, so I feel it is an acceptable form of professional, Broadway-style rehearsing.

It is getting very easy to do a run-through and get everything correct, but now I have to work on character and truthful moments and actually being good in the role. This character is a complex one, and there is a trap to playing him—it is easy to come across as fake. It is easy to fall into a Sopranos stereotype, or fall back on a broader musical theatre stereotype. If I bring one real skill to this job, it is that I am confident in my ability to play scenes truthfully. But it takes some time to get there.

Every actor has their own way of getting to the truth of a scene, and most every actor is trained in at least one of the major techniques. At the risk of trivializing two hundred years of theatre instruction and exploration, I am going to attempt to explain the most commonly used acting methods in three hundred words or less. Take the scene where the band finally decides to buy Tommy out of the group.

- Stanislavski's System: I know my character wants to maintain control of the band, so I will reach my arms out to them and, in doing so, begin to feel the emotion that my reach unleashes within me.

- Strasberg's Method Acting: I know my character wants to maintain control of the band, so I am going to remember what it smelled like the last time I wanted to maintain control of something in my real life and recall that smell while I am onstage.

- The Meisner Technique: I know my character wants to maintain control of the band, but if Frankie says his line on Wednesday night in a way that makes me think maybe I don't want to maintain control after all, then I will give up the idea of maintaining control and react to Frankie in some completely different way than I ever have before.

- The Stella Adler Technique: I know that the author thinks my character wants to maintain control of the band, so I will pretend to tell this to the band in as loud a voice and with as large a hand gesture as I can muster so that it all seems quite epic and grand.

- The Spolin Technique: I know that my character wants to maintain control of the band, but I don't know how to act that out so I am going to play a bunch of fun games with my castmates until somebody tells me that what I did in the game looks cool enough to replicate onstage.

- Suzuki Training: I know that my character wants to maintain control of the band, but I am going to forget about that for a while so that I can do some martial arts and a lot of stomping. When I go back to the show, I will seem more grounded and well-balanced.

- Viewpoints Training: I know that my character wants to maintain control of the band, and it will be cool if I say my lines to the band while following them around onstage, mimicking their gestures, and repeating some of the things they say.

Did my sarcasm register? I hope so. Which method do I use? I like a little from the first and a little from the third.

May 29th, 2009

I come full circle (again) today when I go to the Dodger's rehearsal studio to run the show. This is not a required rehearsal; I asked if I could book the time just to keep the show active in my brain. But the run-through actually gets pretty boring. Can you believe that? I'm rehearsing for my childhood dream, and it gets boring. I know all the stuff I am supposed to know and have learned to do these things correctly, but unless I do them with other people, it's boring.

I have to build a relationship with the other guys onstage and with the audience too. I spend the first twenty minutes of the show talking to the audience and, silly as it sounds, I feel like I need an audience to figure out exactly what that relationship is. Des McAnuff told me early on that the Tommy-Audience relationship is one like buddies at a bar—they are a captive audience but I still need to prove something to them, to defend myself to them. This is a great place to start, but I can't wait for the preview performances to work out the kinks.

Preview performances are those that take place before the official opening night, and are viewed with a bit more leniency than regular performances. They are used to get a feel for what impact an audience has on a show. Oh, wait. *Jersey Boys: Toronto* is already open. I don't get any preview performances. (Damn.)

I have my third costume fitting of the week, heading back to St. Laurie Merchant Tailors to try on my suits.

"Hmm. You've lost weight," the tailor tells me.

"Oh, I wish!" I say while looking down at my belly, which has a few too many pints of beer and late-night nachos floating around in it.

"No, no. You've lost weight. These pants are too big. Even this jacket is too big."

"Oh. Well, honestly, I weigh myself every morning hoping for some good news, but I haven't had any in a long time!"

He is not in the mood for such sarcasm. "Well, clearly you have lost weight because these sizes are just all wrong."

"Maybe the measurements were off?" I suggest, not realizing that telling a tailor that his measurements are off is like telling an actor his motivation is not clear; it insults the fundamentals of the profession.

"Perhaps, perhaps," he says, but he really means, "No, you are dumb."

I don't want to argue anymore and come across as "the annoying actor," but come on. I was just here, what, three weeks ago? The scale in my bathroom says exactly the same thing it did when I left for Orlando. And isn't it physically impossible for a person's shoulders to shrink from a size 42 (like they built) to a size 38 or 40 (like I am and always have been)? I adore having suits made for me, but this is an unsettling trip.

May 30th, 2009

It's my last full day in New York for a long time. Cara comes back home tomorrow after I leave. Mark has been reclusive the past two days, barricading himself in his room most of the time. Is he upset that I am leaving? Or psyched that there will be one less person in the apartment making sure he does his homework? Who knows. I love him, but I am never sure how to approach him. I don't even know how to tell him what I'm thinking right now, which is that it kills me to know I will be away for an entire year of his schooling, and that I know I will not be able to miss another school year after this. No matter how much this dream job means to me, I know I'm going to have to come home soon(ish) to this New York family life I am committed to.

I go to the gym early, then for a run. Double exercise! Gotta be like John Lloyd Young! Then I meet a friend for brunch at Blockhead's, feeling an incredible need to say goodbye to somebody. I used to go out of town for work quite often, but that feels like a lifetime ago and going out of town for a long period now just feels sad. Mark doesn't want to come to brunch with us. No surprise there, I guess. But I wish he would.

And then it is time to pack. Packing is difficult because not only am I packing for a long, long time, but I will be carrying everything myself through the airports and need a manageable system. I end up with a carry-on bag filled with shirts, a duffel bag with pants and shoes, a backpack with my vocal score, scripts, dramaturgy, and day planner, and a guitar case stuffed full of underwear. Yes. I have to fill the extra space in my guitar case with underwear because there is no room for it anywhere else. (And what am I going to wear while rehearsing by myself if I don't have lots of underwear?)

Ready to go. I guess. This dream job is much less exciting when all my bags are packed.

REHEARSING IN TORONTO (AGAIN)

SUBWAY CARDS, QUICK-CHANGES, & NINE-IRONS

May 31st, 2009

The morning starts with a sweaty walk to Penn Station, carrying the means to work and live for the next year on my back. I take the New Jersey Transit train out to Newark International Airport. Riding the train on this route, I pass through Belleville, New Jersey, boyhood home of Tommy DeVito and site of the Four Seasons' beginnings. I pass the famous industrial New Jersey skyline that features as a backdrop on the *Jersey Boys* set. And I pass the long Goethals Bridge that is supposed to be conjured by the metal trusses on the set. I am on my way.

The airline I take departs from a small terminal. Porter Airlines is a Toronto-based company and they share the terminal with El Al Airlines, which offers non-stop flights to Tel Aviv. Frankly, Canada and Israel feel equally far away today. And the terminal is so tiny that they warn me there is no coffee beyond the security checkpoint. Do I really look that tired?

Upon arriving in Toronto, I take a cab to my temporary lodgings. I am staying about a half-hour south of the theatre (too far) and about a fifteen-minute walk from the subway station (also too far). Oh, well. It is only temporary, and the apartment is extremely large. The building feels like a retirement complex and, come to think of it, probably is a retirement complex. (There are VHS tapes in the lobby that residents can borrow. 'Nuf said.) The large common room has a pond in it that is filled with gigantic goldfish. Rachel will dig that when she gets here.

I want to settle in to my new city before the craziness of the next couple weeks, so I unpack and go for a long run in the surrounding neighborhoods. This part of Toronto is very residential. It's nice enough, but not particularly exciting. I run along many streets with houses, one with apartment buildings, over some train tracks, through a cemetery, past the supermarket…and I could have been in any town anywhere in North America. Nothing distinctive here. Rock music, standing ovations, and my name in lights are a half-hour north.

I am not nervous about the show, really, but I am anxious about this new life away from home. I get lonely. Really lonely. I am glad to have a wife who doesn't mind a million short phone calls a day. But even some of those phone calls end up being hard.

"Daniel, I'm home now and your clothes are gone." Cara is feeling alone now that she arrived back in New York.

"Not all of them, hon."

"No, just the ones you actually wear." I can't argue there.

So I ask, "How's Mark?"

"He's fine. But he's not talking to me."

"Yeah, he wasn't talking to me much either."

"I guess he's just processing the changes we are making around here."

I get defensive. "We're not making any changes, Cara, I'm just doing a new job for a while. It's not forever. And you'll be up here before you know it."

"No, I'll be here and you'll be there. Don't get me wrong; I'm still happy and I know this is the best thing for you, but I can't tell you it's not killing me to not have anyone to eat with right now." Note that Cara isn't complaining about not having someone to talk with, walk with, or sleep with. Just eat with.

It is 11:00 p.m. We often eat nachos at 11:00 p.m. This neighborhood in Toronto seems to have nowhere to eat at night except one gross little dive bar.

That's not going to be good for my routine.

June 1st, 2009

Today sucks. Only two places here allow you to buy a monthly subway pass with a credit card, and one of those places is sold out of the passes today. I literally spend an hour trying to buy a card. How can you have a city with a public transit system that doesn't let me give it money? I want to buy a (very expensive) monthly subway card, you send me all over the place to do it, and then you are sold out of them? How is that even possible? When I finally get to the place that sells cards and has them in stock, there are only two credit card machines and one of them is broken. The line at the only working machine is thirty people deep. I ask you, what is the purpose of a public transit system? To let people get around the city more efficiently, right? So how is it efficient if it takes me an hour to get a monthly pass? This is the most ludicrous thing I have ever experienced.

And Verizon's service in this country gets me angry, too. I pay a lot of money now for a Family Plan that includes coverage in both the United States and Canada. But guess what? First, the coverage here in northern Toronto is lousy. Second, searching for coverage drains the battery on my phone incredibly fast and I can't go a full day without charging it. Third, my phone doesn't ring in this country! I'm sure this last one is a problem that can be fixed, but ever since I crossed the border my phone will show someone is calling, but refuses to ring or vibrate. So I'm missing calls from Cara all the time. And it kills me.

I go for a run to clear my head of the subway pass situation, then for a three-hour walk in the evening to explore downtown Toronto. (I'm really committing to this exercise, huh? The *Jersey Boys* workout regime! Oh wait, is this effecting my suit size?) Downtown Toronto seems cool enough. The blocks are long, and streetcars carry people east-west while the major subway line travels north-south. The subway seems much less frequent than I am used to in New York, but I guess this is because most people still seem to drive here. (It's been a long time since I have driven with any consistency.)

Toronto seems much, much dirtier than New York, but there is a reason for this: the city is in the midst of a sanitation workers strike and the raw garbage is piling up everywhere. Welcome to my new home! Every public trashcan has a pile of garbage built around it, and some public parks are being used as temporary garbage-collection stations. Trash bags are dumped in these parks until they reach twenty feet high. And there are rats. I know this is not the normal state of being for this ordinarily beautiful city on the lakefront, but I find it hard not to have a really awful first impression. I am looking forward to starting work again tomorrow, just so I can be inside all day.

June 2nd, 2009

I get to try on some of my costumes this morning, but those suits that didn't fit last time are suspiciously absent from the fitting. The wardrobe department at the theatre (ten people in all) seems to be full of terrific personalities. These are people who have worked together for a long time; they do puzzles during intermission and take turns baking desserts to share. Their large room, the largest wardrobe room I have ever seen actually, is lit with Christmas and Halloween lights. (It's June.)

Upon trying on some blue pants, the head of wardrobe tells me, "Dan, you look great in these!" I think she likes the fresh, unwashed color in the fabric. (I think. But it is quite possible she was looking directly at my butt when she delivered the compliment. My butt does look quite good in the blue pants.)

"Yeah, they're terrific," I say, "but I bet I will never see them on me again." I wear the costumes too quickly in the show to ever get a chance to look in a mirror.

I have a spacing rehearsal during the day with two people I will be getting a lot of notes from in the next month: the production stage manager, Cindy Toushan, and the dance captain, Victoria Lamond. Both are very clearly on my side today. Even though the rehearsal is an easy one, just working through any differences between what I was taught and what actually occurs in the Toronto production, they are both full of compliments. I know where I am supposed to be, and I do a smash-up job walking casually through the show.

I visit the hair room for a haircut. I have been growing my hair since I was offered this role, and it is getting quite out of control. They cut it short on the sides, help me figure out an appropriate (greasy) style, and dye it almost black!

I'm supposed to look more Italian now, but still I say there are blond Italians, right? And Tommy DeVito himself didn't have hair that was very dark. Oh, well. It does make for a striking look. My eyebrows are still very blond, though. Black hair. Pasty blond eyebrows. There's a joke in there somewhere.

I had my hair cut today because there is a scheduled photo call. With a new lead actor in the show, the company prints all new brochures, advertisements, lobby photos, and even a giant billboard outside. These pictures are all being done today, so the cast begins arriving for them in the early evening, greeting me in less dramatic fashion than last time I was in town. The photo call itself has many people doting on me. And those lights! My first time standing under full light on the stage and I find it absolutely blinding. I am not exaggerating when I say that I can't see two feet in front of me. I can't even see the two feet attached to me.

I watch the show this evening from a box on the side of the theatre and am struck again by the power *Jersey Boys* has. The audiences in New York and Florida were loud and fun right from the first moments of the show, but the Toronto audience has a different flavor, one that proves the show's worth. This Toronto audience starts off far more reserved than the other two types I have observed. Perhaps because of the influence of the Stratford and Shaw Festivals (theatre organizations with more of a classical influence), this audience seems hesitant to clap or laugh too loudly. While they enjoy themselves from the first moments of the show, they do not vocalize their enjoyment as much as I have seen in the other cities. But here's the thing: I can actually hear them get louder with each successive scene; and by the time the big numbers in the second act come along they are screaming and jumping to their feet. It is like the show has lifted them up, one song at a time, until they can no longer stay in their seats. They go on such a ride that they seem to absolutely burst with excitement during the finale. It is amazing to watch. This Toronto audience is not an easy sell, but they are always sold by the end of the evening.

I finish my night with a long subway ride to my temporary neighborhood, a solitary dinner at the only place that still serves food at this time of night, a long walk up to my apartment, and a too-short conversation with Cara as she falls asleep. It is easy to feel lonely here.

June 3rd, 2009

There are two shows for the cast today, and I am given the choice of how to spend my time. I have not run through the show in real time since Orlando, so I ask if there is a place I can set up and run the show while listening to it over the monitors. Not only is there a place, but it is an infinitely better place than my wardrobe room setup down in Florida. They let me take over an entire small theatre, one that adjoins the larger auditorium where *Jersey Boys* resides. An electrician rigs the small stage monitor so it will play through a larger speaker in my personal theatre, and he installs a television that is cabled through to the adjoining building so I can see the live performance as well. Unbelievable.

They give me a few guitars to use, some basic props, and even a swing. That's right. One of the swings not performing this afternoon runs through the show with me, playing all the other parts himself. Grant Tilly covers six roles in the show, and knows all the nuances of each actor. He is even able to give me a whole lot of information about my own track, because he has already performed it about twenty times.

Grant helps a lot; he finds the perfect balance of respecting my own differences and helping me with what the other actors are used to. It's quite tricky to do. I'm sure he notices a bunch of things that I do differently, or even wrong, but he is very careful about what he says and how he says it so that he isn't telling me what to do. I like him right away, and am in awe of his knowledge about the subtler points of doing this role. He teaches me which pocket to keep my prop car keys in, when to transfer the deck of cards from my jacket pocket to my pants pocket, where to keep water bottles backstage, and a million necessary tidbits like that.

During my dinner break, I opt to stay at the theatre and work on some of the guitar parts. I play the songs decently now, but am still figuring out which ones I trust my playing enough to have the guitar turned on for. Playing guitar while dancing is like writing a letter while walking. You can do it, but it comes out messy. (To make an even more accurate comparison,

111

try writing the letter while running, dodging taxicabs, and holding a cup of coffee; that's what it's like playing guitar while dancing in *Jersey Boys*.)

June 4th, 2009

Oh, What a Day! The entire cast is called into the rehearsal studio with me today so we can work through the show together for the first time. It is hard on my brain, but absolutely thrillingly and breathtakingly fun.

With long studio mirrors in front of us, we all take our places for the top of the show. We have just a piano for accompaniment, and no costumes or microphones, but every other element was brought into the rehearsal room and is waiting for me: my real guitars, props, microphone stands set to my height, tables, and chairs. And the cast seems excited.

My opening position is hanging on a fence, but of course there is no fence in the rehearsal room, so I mime holding a fence during the first number. Then, my entrance music begins and the rest of the show barrels on like the freight train it is.

What do I remember? I remember my hands shaking as I sang "Silhouettes," and I kept hoping no one would notice. I remember the scene change into "Apple Of My Eye" happening smoothly all around me, and a guitar virtually appearing in my hands as the scene change ended and the song began. I remember another thrilling version of "Cry For Me" because I was hearing these guys—my guys—for the first time. I remember sweating so much during the Big Three that I couldn't hold on to my guitar pick. And I remember lots of congratulations from the cast.

I do all right with this run; I was not great, but they all congratulate me as if it was a success. Good people.

I go to dinner at a local barbecue joint with some of the cast. Here's a thing I am realizing about this area: the cast members of *Jersey Boys* get special treatment when they eat at local restaurants, and other patrons recognize them when they come in the door. This is a crazy feeling.

Michael Lomenda, Jeff Madden, Quinn VanAntwerp, Daniel Robert Sullivan
©Joan Marcus

Daniel Robert Sullivan, Jeff Madden, Quinn VanAntwerp, Michael Lomenda
©Joan Marcus

I watch the show this evening and take notes. I am trying to be very specific in noticing what Jeremy Kushnier does. As I mentioned before, there is no way to copy another actor's performance and have it seem truthful. But there is something to be said for taking lots of what Jeremy does and making my own version of it, for the cast is used to his rhythms and certain of his moments. I am going to change things a lot here, but I am trying to keep the general rhythms and timings the same. So, my notebook is full of things like, "Say second speech slower than I have been," "Respond to Frankie right away during every line of first scene—no air in between," and "Put a lot of space before saying 'what' in bowling alley scene." I have learned a lot from watching other guys play this role (Christian, Jeremy, Matt, Dominic). I tip my hat to them.

And the best part about tonight? My director from New York, Shelley Butler, arrived. After being away from any kind of artistic direction for weeks now, it will be nice to have her here again. I know the moves now. I know the lines now. And I know what I'm supposed to sing. Now, she will provide the discerning eye to make what I'm doing seem good and believable. Or she'll tell them to fire me.

June 5th, 2009

This is a high-energy day. We work onstage with the full cast, props, and set. We have no band yet, just a piano for accompaniment. This is my first time moving pieces like the car seats and the whore bench on our actual set, and I find it difficult once again to find the proper marks on the floor. It looks like a landing strip for clowns—lots of marks in lots of colors. (Afterthought: "Landing strip for clowns" is not a great metaphor, but it is my honest first thought when I see the stage up close for the first time.) I also discover that I have to be very careful wheeling the whore bench out from the wings because the actress playing Mary Delgado sits on the bench with her hand slightly off the edge and I come very close to scraping her hand against the metal poles on the set.

114

The work-through goes well enough, but all I can think is that this rehearsal process is backward, with me learning the steps and technical elements before really even knowing how to play Tommy DeVito, the person. I am still not sure how to perform him well. And I open in eleven days!

Eleven days. Hmm. That actually seems like a good amount of time. I have mounted many shows in summer stock in two weeks or less. I even mounted a show in two days once. (Each of us in the show had done our respective roles before, so there was no new material to learn, but still...two days! We arrived in town and met each other for the first time on Sunday night, and then opened the show on the following Tuesday night.) So, eleven days left should be no problem. I should be fine building a solid, believable character in eleven days. Right? Right.

The show really is a tidy knot of perfection. There isn't too much room for playing, improvising, or really doing anything other than the specific things I am told to do. But I find myself wishing I had more time devoted strictly to character work. I am lucky. Shelley thinks the same thing.

Instead of watching the cast's evening performance, Shelley and I go into the rehearsal studio and work over all of the direct addresses Tommy gives to the audience in the first half of the show. We work on the way he brags right out of the gate. We work on finding a bit of a smirk. We work on figuring out the fine line between playing smart and playing dumb. This last one proves tricky. Tommy has a lot of lines in the show that come off as being a little dense, stupid even. But he also has some very slick, very witty lines that a "stupid" person wouldn't come up with. So, I have to find the proper balance.

For some reason, I also start to freak out tonight that I will forget my lines during one of my first performances. This is idiotic. I have not forgotten my lines once yet, and I rehearse the entire show every single day. But I am thinking about character today instead of the technical aspects, and freeing my brain like that makes me have to trust that the words will come...but what if they didn't? Tommy begins the show with twenty minutes of solo speeches to the audience. What if I were to launch into the wrong speech? That would be easy to do. Every speech feels the same because the spotlight is bright and I am in my own little bubble. If I were to begin the wrong speech, I am not even sure I would know it was wrong until I finished.

Many people have the impression that if an actor forgets a line they need simply whisper offstage to have someone cue them, but this is completely untrue. Were I to forget a line, I would be completely and utterly alone in trying to salvage the situation. There is no such thing as a "prompter" in the theatre. My options would be to say any of the following:

- "And you know something else? No? Well, I don't either." (Then exit the stage.)
- "And that's all I have to say about that." (Then exit the stage.)
- "Look back there!" (Then point to the back of the audience and exit the stage.)

At the end of rehearsal, I have a particularly dramaturgical conversation with Shelley, and I adore dramaturgical conversations. I heard it said that Tommy doesn't change much by the end of *Jersey Boys*, that he remains the self-centered schemer that he is at the beginning. I have always believed, however, that every major character in literature and theatre has to undergo a transformation, that it is a prerequisite to being a major character in the first place. So, I believe Tommy changes. In real life, Tommy DeVito married his long-time girlfriend and reaffirmed his faith in Christianity. I believe the authors of *Jersey Boys* represent this change in the script by having Tommy acknowledge the loss of Frankie's daughter (a heartfelt moment), and I feel I can accentuate the change by wearing a wedding ring in the final scene. Shelley buys this argument. And I feel good to have brought it up.

I ride the subway downtown with Michael Lomenda, who plays Nick Massi in the show. I have a lot of scenes with him, but this subway ride is the first time we have ever really spoken. He seems like a terrific guy. He, Quinn, and Jeff Madden (who plays Frankie) are taking Jeremy out for a final night on the town this Sunday. They have rented a limo for seven hours, and are going to hit all the classy places in the city, including the bar at the top of the CN Tower. I have to admit, I have a secret desire to be invited. I shouldn't be invited, as it is their last time together and they are a tight unit, but I still hope I will be. I want to hang out with them, get to know them, and feel like a part of the group. Sunday is also the Tony Awards broadcast, but I think I would give up watching the Tony Awards to hang out with them. And I always watch the Tony Awards.

June 6th, 2009

I spend the cast's first show of the day trailing Jeremy backstage and discover that he is a real ball-buster. Not a second goes by back there that he is not smacking another actor, chasing a musician, singing a funny song to a dresser, throwing guitar picks at a stagehand, or flicking a towel at...well...anybody. And this all occurs just moments before he steps onstage to sing the next song. He is a personality to contend with, for sure. And he keeps things active and fun. He's done the show for two years, so I guess this is one way to keep himself, and everyone else, in the game.

No one in the show has time to go to their dressing rooms to change costumes. This was true with the National Tour and remains true here in Toronto. And the quick-change into the Big Three, a change that I witnessed once before and knew would be tricky, actually happens as four quick-changes right next to each other. I didn't realize this before. The Four Seasons line up next to each other with four dressers ready to go. The dressers help rip off shirts, Velcro up new ones, slip on jackets, and push the Seasons back onstage. Seeing this group of eight people work so swiftly and precisely is great fun. It is a backstage ballet. And if something goes wrong, I have a feeling "Sherry" will start without them.

It is also fun to see one of our stage managers, Melanie Klodt, call the show today. She dances through many of the pages, calling the cues on beats of the music as she wiggles around. I have never seen a stage manager dance before, so it must be the effect of the music. There are some shows that you get sick of hearing the music, shows where you turn down the dressing room monitors so you don't have to hear the songs when you are not onstage. But there are some shows where the music is genuinely catchy, powerful, or engaging and you rarely tire of hearing it. I'm starting to think that *Jersey Boys* falls into the latter category, and that this explains why the Four Seasons have sold more than 175 million records.

Casting Director Merri Sugarman arrives this evening from New York, causing quite a stir. She is here in town to cast a replacement for one of the female roles, as one of the actresses is on medical leave and the only female

117

swing has been covering the part every day for too long now. I notice tonight how my relationship with Merri has changed. Now that I am in the *Jersey Boys* family, we are buddies and can talk about all kinds of things. It is like I have crossed the line from being the person who walks in the audition room very respectfully and does everything she says to being just another friend from work.

Although I have no actual rehearsal today, just trailing Jeremy and watching the second show, I do discover something funny about yesterday's rehearsal. Fake marijuana joints are used in the show, and since I don't smoke I have been practicing inhaling with them. Stage management gave me a bunch of (very fat) joints to rehearse with and I mistakenly left two of them on a table in the rehearsal studio. A children's theatre group rehearsed in that same studio this morning. And yes, a child found the joints, brought them to his director, and asked what they were! They were turned over to security, for the director assumed they were actual marijuana joints. Woops.

June 7th, 2009

Based on my work two days ago, I have an hour of notes with Victoria, the dance captain. And I thought the notes were specific before! Now, they are even more so.

"Dan, your guitar should be at 60° instead of 80°."

"Um, ok."

"Dan, your body should be at 45° around the microphone stand instead of 30°."

"Um, sure."

"Dan, your hands should actually touch your legs after the snaps, not just come close to touching your legs."

"No problem."

"Dan, you have to pull your guitar neck back beyond your shoulder instead of just to your shoulder."

"Of course."

"Dan, your head should snap to the right on the first count of the second eight, instead of the last count of the first eight."

"Is that a change generated by Meisner's technique, or Stanislavski's?"

"Huh?"

"Never mind."

No excuses anymore, I guess. And before I get sarcastic again, I think I should remind myself that actors have been fired from this production for not being up to par. I do not want to be fired for not being up to par.

Later, I make a call about an apartment. I have to leave the retirement complex I am currently living in by the end of the month, and I am starting to spend my free time (ha! free time!) looking for a new place that is nice enough to spend a year in and big enough to have Cara and the kids with me part of the time. I was given the phone number of Lindsay Thomas' boyfriend. Lindsay is the cast member on medical leave, and her apartment directly next door to the theatre is becoming vacant. Her boyfriend makes plans to show me the place tomorrow.

I head home on the subway and, again, have dinner by myself at the dive in my neighborhood. The four *Jersey Boys* are doing their night on the town to say goodbye to Jeremy tonight, and I was not invited as I had secretly hoped. I told myself that I should not have been invited and it would have been weird to have me there, but still I harbored the secret wish! So, to the Tony Awards I go. Well, to my television I go, rushing back from dinner to catch the opening sequence.

Although *Jersey Boys* isn't eligible for awards this year, they do have a featured performance. The performance is "Can't Take My Eyes Off Of You" in which five of the actors playing Frankie Valli from across North America each sing a section. While they sing, the city in which they are performing flashes on a giant screen behind them: Las Vegas, Chicago, National Tour, New York, and Toronto. Wait. Toronto?

It turns out that our Frankie Valli, being the only actor from outside of the United States, is not able to participate in this performance because the producers couldn't get work papers processed for him in time. So, the Toronto Frankie that shows up on the broadcast is actually the National Tour Frankie (justified because the National Tour played Toronto last year before the Toronto Company took over), and the National Tour Frankie that shows is actually the National Tour Joe Pesci. You get all that?

119

That is a disappointment, and maybe one of the reasons our Frankie, Jeff Madden, is going out tonight instead of staying home and watching the Tonys himself. He is an amazing actor, one who brings more depth to the role of Frankie Valli than I would have thought possible. And Jeff just won a Dora Award for the role, the Canadian equivalent to a Tony Award.

The Tony Awards have always been a special night for me. As a kid who loved theatre, the only way I knew what was going on in the professional theatre world was by watching the Tony Awards. Each performance was a three-minute glimpse into what was happening in those grand, mysterious theatres off in the magical city that I had not yet visited: New York. There will always be kids watching the Tonys and dreaming about one day being a part of them. I taped the Tonys every year and memorized all of the performances. I can still tell you what songs were performed from each nominated musical from about 1988 until today. I was proud to be the only person I knew who had these broadcasts on tape and could watch them whenever I wanted. Imagine my disappointment when the website BlueGobo.com came along with a vast archive that let everyone in the world see these same broadcasts. My VHS tapes are no longer valuable, but I still keep them under my bed. Damn that BlueGobo. Damn that Al Gore and his internet.

June 8th, 2009

Today is a day off, so I spend it hunting for an apartment. I begin by looking at buildings down on the waterfront. (Ok, maybe I begin with a luxury side trip to the top of the CN Tower. What a place! It is over a hundred stories tall and has a glass floor way up there near the top. I am so nervous to step on that floor that I spend most of the time just sort of tapping it with my foot to make sure it is sturdy. It is sturdy enough for the five-year-old tap-dancing on it, but not for me.)

The waterfront apartments are all beautiful buildings with lake views and bowling alleys in the basement. New York hardly has bowling alleys in the city, never mind in an apartment building's basement. The commute down here takes about forty-five minutes from the theatre, and I am not sure I want to live that far away. Although, having people recognize me on the subway ride after a show would be very good for my ego. But that shouldn't be a deciding factor in choosing an apartment, should it? (Should it?) So I travel back up north to the theatre and look at a few apartments in the surrounding block. They are cheaper here, but the neighborhood is not nearly as interesting. But if I am going to have the family here with me for the summer, I want them to be a presence at the theatre. They will not be a presence at the theatre if they have to travel forty-five minutes from the waterfront just to get here.

I visit with Lindsay's boyfriend and see her apartment next door to the theatre. Her balcony overlooks the stage door from many stories in the air. It is a beautiful place, but I think too small for my family.

Later, Cara calls after some small argument with Mark, needing some consolation. "I feel like a single parent again," she says.

"But you are not a single parent, hon. I am here with my phone on, just like always. I can talk to you anytime you need me."

"It's not the same."

And she's right. It's not the same.

June 9th, 2009

A two-hour choreography rehearsal with Caitlin Carter leaves me sweating through my shirt. She arrived earlier today, and I realize I hadn't seen her since she taught me the first four or five numbers back in New York. She leaves little room for error, and little room for breathing! She will be here in Toronto for at least a week, maybe more. And her job is...um...me.

I follow that sweaty dance extravaganza with an hour with Shelley. The work goes well, but I really need other guys in the room to act with. (Haven't I said this before?) I act these scenes just fine with imaginary partners, because imaginary partners do exactly what I want them to do. Real actors tend to be less predictable.

121

"Daniel, I know things will change when you get other guys in these scenes with you."

"Oh, yeah, I'm sure of it," I tell her. "I just wish it could happen now."

"Well, that's just a money thing. They can only afford to pay for so much overtime. Think of it as a compliment! We don't think you need the extra rehearsal."

I watch the evening show with Shelley and Caitlin and get an earful of commentary about what people are doing. They have seen this show, and its many variations, countless times. They laugh at choices that are different than expected, and then decide whether "different" is bad or just different. Usually, it seems, different is just different, although there are definitely places where they expect certain things to remain identical in all the companies. (I take mental note of these places so I can squelch any future inspirations.)

After the show, at about 11:00 p.m., I go to see another apartment in the theatre's neighborhood. The guy showing me the place flips out when I tell him I am in *Jersey Boys*, and offers me $100 less rent per month because of it. This is the tiniest taste of celebrity, and I like it. I hope this is a trend. Too bad the apartment smells like feet, and a tiny celebrity can't live in an apartment that smells like feet.

June 10th, 2009

Another two-show day for the cast means another light rehearsal day for me. I watch the first show, rehearsing it only in my head. This proves equally as effective as exercising only in my head.

I go to see two more apartments, both of which are awful. I decided to live up here by the theatre, but every place I see is unlivable.

Then, I come back to the theatre for a quick-change rehearsal. The eight-person quick-change into the Big Three is something easily handled, but the change into "I'm In The Mood For Love" requires practice. So we practice. It isn't perfect, but we make it in time because the two dressers helping me are so good. On a typical night, here is how this change breaks down:

• At 8:33:04, I exit Stage Right in a run, removing my tie clip and placing it my pocket as I approach the two dressers waiting for me.

122

- At 8:33:11, I remove my tie and slip off my shoes, throwing the tie on the ground and leaving the shoes for the dresser in front of me to line up in front of my feet again.
- At 8:33:14, I unbutton my pants and shirt.
- At 8:33:18, the dresser behind me pulls off my shirt.
- At 8:33:21, I pull off my pants.
- At 8:33:24, the dresser behind me holds up a new shirt for me to slide my arms into.
- At 8:33:29, the dresser in front of me holds up a new pair of pants for me to slide into.
- At 8:33:33, I button my pants as the dresser in front of me uses a shoehorn to guide my feet into my shoes again.
- At 8:33:37, I reach to my right for a drink of water, while both dressers button up my shirt, one starting at the top and one at the bottom.
- At 8:33:42, I leave the dressing area and jog over to where the actor playing Nick is holding my guitar for me, the strap open so I can slide it right over my head.
- At 8:34:02, after a few seconds to catch my breath, Nick and I enter the scene and accompany Frankie as he sings, "I'm In The Mood For Love."

The whole process has taken fifty-eight seconds.

After this amazing quick-change work, I run some choreography in an area of the Performing Arts Centre that is above an open kitchen and dining room. It is a bit awkward to be dancing with my guitar while people eat shrimp and asparagus twenty feet below me. I really have rehearsed this show in many settings, haven't I? I've rehearsed at the Dodger's rehearsal space, Adam Ben-David's apartment on the Upper West Side, my bedroom in Midtown, the exercise room in my apartment building, my hotel room in Florida, the stilt-walker's studio, my makeshift wardrobe room rehearsal space in Florida, the stage of the Bob Carr Performing Arts Centre, the rehearsal studio here in Toronto, the Studio Theatre here in Toronto, the stage of the Toronto Centre for the Performing Arts, my apartment here in Toronto, and today, this space above the kitchen. Whew!

After rehearsal, six people work on various parts of my costumes. My suits have arrived. They need more adjusting.

June 11th, 2009

Today is my dress rehearsal. It is my first time in costume, my first time with a microphone (we wear two, actually, in case one breaks), and my first time with the band. What a ride it is.

Michael Lomenda, Daniel Robert Sullivan, Jeff Madden, Quinn VanAntwerp
©Joan Marcus

I learn, and re-learn, many things. For example, I learn that Tommy needs an attack right out of the gate, but that this attack needs to be calm, cool, and collected. Today, I am not at all calm, not at all cool, and not at all collected. I am high on adrenaline, and attack out of the gate too harshly. How do I fix that? I guess onstage repetition is the way, because the rehearsal room just cannot duplicate the

124

adrenaline rush of hearing the band kick in and seeing the spotlights turn on as I slide downstage for my first entrance. The more I experience that moment, the more calm, cool, and collected I will become.

The sound mix differs greatly from what I'm used to hearing in the audience. Onstage, I hear more voices than music, so I can tune to other people but not to the band. That said, hearing more voices really lets me dig into the harmony, and "Cry For Me" is thrilling as always.

The eight-person costume change leading into "Sherry" doesn't go so well. This is supposed to be the easy quick-change, the one that didn't require any rehearsal, but I get caught up in the Velcro and don't make the change in time. I run onstage with my guitar around my neck, but my pants around my knees.

Throughout the first half of the show, my microphone cord keeps getting caught in my waist and pulling down on my hair. We wear two microphones threaded through our hair and running down to two transmitters strapped in a belt around our chest. This is standard and I have worn such a rig countless times in my life. But I have never worn pants that were so high-waisted! Seriously, the pants in this show make me feel like Grandpa Joe from *Willy Wonka*. So the cord drifts down, gets caught in the high waist of my pants, and pulls my head back. If you ever see a Jersey Boy not moving his head, you now know why. Blame it on his old-fashioned pants.

Between shows, with no rest for the weary, I go to visit three lousy apartments, then return to receive notes from Shelley and Caitlin. My choreography notes are simple and don't disappointment me too much (because I didn't disappoint Caitlin too much). But my acting notes are not too positive with regards to the opening speeches. Tommy sets the tone for the show; if I am too frantic, then the entire show will seem frantic. I have always been good at sensing an audience and talking to them directly in a settled tone, but the spotlights won't even let me see the audience in this show. How can I talk to them if I can't see them?

Oh my, I am exhausted. My joints hurt. My bones hurt. I even think my bone marrow hurts. Good night, Cara. I miss you. But even if you were here, I would still be going to bed right this second.

June 12th, 2009

Well, this is it! The day of my put-in rehearsal. The infamous day that every replacement actor prepares for. (Oh, what am I talking about? I have never been a replacement actor. I just feel like I have because "the new guy" seems to be my full identity these days.)

A put-in rehearsal is the only time a new actor gets to do a complete version of the show before performing it in front of an audience. It's the only time when everyone is in costume with me, all the lights are on, and we are not supposed to stop to fix any mistakes. It's a rehearsal that is supposed to mimic a real performance exactly.

The cast is warmed up and ready to go. There is a photographer present taking pictures for press releases and the like. And I do pretty well, infinitely better than yesterday. Shelley gave me so many notes yesterday on toughening up my Tommy that I come in ready to be a cocky jerk. (Well, to play a cocky jerk, not to be a cocky jerk. If I decided to be a cocky jerk I might get fired, and being fired is still very much a fear I am trying to deal with.) I maintain my sarcastic smile and jokester attitude, but I add a layer of "confident braggart." I think it works.

I try to speak to the audience with confidence and authority, but the only audience present is Shelley, Caitlin, the photographer, and a couple of cleaning ladies who are clearly judging me.

My big technical issue of the day is what to do with my many guitar picks. Sometimes I need them in my pocket, sometimes attached to the guitar, sometimes they need to just go away, and I have to figure out how to make all that happen. I am currently playing "Apple Of My Eye," "I Go Ape," and "My Mother's Eyes" with the guitar turned on, and "Cry For Me," "Big Girls Don't Cry," "Walk Like A Man," "Dawn," "Big Man In Town," and "Beggin" with the guitar turned off. I am completely faking "I Can't Give You Anything For Love," "I'm In The Mood For Love," and "Sherry." I look forward to shifting those categories a bit in the next month.

After the rehearsal, Shelley says, "Daniel, you were a total ass." So I think I succeeded. But my hands were still shaking at the beginning.

June 13th, 2009

Time is running out. I begin my morning with an hour of vocal rehearsal with our musical director. I usually try to sing with a fuller sound, but this rehearsal is all about trying to get the sound brighter by putting it forward in my nose. A good vocal blend happens not necessarily when singers have individually terrific voices, but when they have good voices that sound similar. For this reason an oboe and a trumpet will never blend as well as an oboe and a clarinet. Similarly, my brother (who is a firefighter and will be mad at me for putting this in print) sounded amazing harmonizing "The First Noel" in the car with me while we were growing up, even though he is not really a singer. But it sounded good because his voice is similar to mine. The singers in this show have a more forward sound, so I need to have a more forward sound.

Later, when checking in with stage management about where I should be, they suggest I take the night off. Really? Do I look like I need a break or something?

For the first time I have no real obligation here in Toronto. I feel like I know the show as well as I am going to, so I jump on the subway and go down to the waterfront. The waterfront is Toronto's place of beauty. A mid-city meditation. Away from the trash that has piled up in the city parks, and the bad apartments I have seen up by the theatre, the lake is calm and refreshing. I take a long walk just to relax, vow to get on a boat as soon as possible, and then come back here to my apartment to sit on the couch and cement myself for the night. I Facebook everyone in the cast. It was Cara's idea to wait until tonight to do this.

"Daniel, you don't want to seem desperate by friending everyone on Facebook the first day you get to Canada. You don't even know them yet."

"But how am I going to get to know them if I don't friend them on Facebook?"

"Well, you could talk to them."

"Cara, talking to somebody is just not the same as friending them on Facebook. When I talk to them, they don't show me their pictures, tell me their status updates, say who they are in a relationship with, or what their political views are..."

Such is our modern world.

June 14th, 2009

There is a lot of excitement at the theatre today because Jeremy will perform as Tommy for the last time. Before it begins, I have an hour of choreography work with Caitlin, although I mostly just run things without much commentary from her. I choose to view her lack of notes as a good sign, a sign that I am exactly where I should be with only two days before opening. (Oh my. Two days before opening. It is getting hard to be cool about all of this. I want to shout, "TWO DAYS! HOLY COW! TWO DAYS UNTIL I GET TO STAR IN THIS FREAKIN' HOT SHOW!" But instead I have to remain calm and say things like, "I have truly enjoyed this rehearsal process very much, thank you.")

Later, I go to a costume fitting to see how my pants are shaping up. Not too well, since they continue to take them in. I ask if it would be helpful if I ate more doughnuts.

I go into the theatre to watch Jeremy's final moments onstage. And what moments they are! He plays the show with the same solid focus as always, but at the curtain call there is a full five-minute standing ovation just for him. Although he works a lot in New York, he is actually Canadian by birth and this is a fitting goodbye. He tears up, and so do some of the other guys up there with him. Girlie men, all of them.

PAUSE FOR COMEDIC EFFECT

Just kidding. I was tearing up, too.

Following the show, we attend a going-away party for Jeremy at a restaurant across the street. Our guitar player, Levon, screens a video for Jeremy in which many, many people say some kind of goodbye. Even I am in the video, my goodbye (scripted by Levon) is something like, "Hey, you've been doing this show for two years now. It's about time you fucking left and let somebody else get a job." I am getting more used to saying the f-word. *Jersey Boys* will do that to you. I never used to swear before, but now I swear at least five times a day and am 100% certain that number will be increasing in the coming weeks. (Mom, please ignore this last paragraph.)

One of the stagehands was videotaped telling Jeremy to "teach the new guy how to swing a golf club before you leave." There is a point in the show where Tommy swings a club and I guess this stagehand thinks I am not doing it well. I have to be honest here and say this really embarrasses me in front of the large group. I know he was acting in good fun, but the awkward silence that follows his line shows me that everyone feels weird about it. And now everyone will be checking out my golf swing on opening night.

Jeff Madden's wife and kids are here, so I meet them for the first time. Beautiful, all of them. And Grant Tilly invites me into his building near the theatre to look at the bulletin board of vacancy listings. I love this building! I call one of the owners and am able to see an apartment right away. It is a two bedroom apartment on the 37th floor with floor-to-ceiling windows in every room looking all the way down to the lake. Incredible. I want this place. I take pictures and, assuming Cara thinks it's a good choice (how could she not?) I will put money down on it tomorrow.

And you know what I'm going to do now? I'm going to watch YouTube videos on how to properly swing a nine-iron.

June 15th, 2009

Today is a day off, but a day off before opening night is kind of like a scenic plane ride before skydiving.

I sleep as long as I can force myself to, but the sun streaming in and a pile of nervous energy makes it difficult. I go for a run and get hopelessly lost. Toronto is full of ravines; ravines that are wooded and filled with great paths. The only problem is the paths are not in straight lines and when you come up out of the ravine you can appear in a completely unrecognizable part of the city. My intended half-hour run turns into two hours. (I hope my pants still fit.)

I go to the drugstore and buy lots of Gatorade. Let's get personal for a second; I've been feeling dehydrated during rehearsals and I'm looking for an alternative to slurping tons of water. The quantities of water I feel I need are filling my bladder far too quickly, and there is only one quick chance to use the

129

restroom in the first act (just after "Oh, What A Night"). One pair of pants I wear in the show is not so high-waisted and sits just below my belly button, right on my bladder. My bladder was so full the other day that these pants popped open just as I entered the stage. There is a bit too much subtext happening when Tommy makes an entrance buttoning up his pants...

While at the store, I buy a fun Canada mug for Rachel. Tomorrow will be her first time in a new country.

After cleaning the apartment a little, I go out to buy some small thank-you gifts for the cast and crew. I thought it might be fun to get bottles of sherry at the liquor store, so I buy five cases of them. The clerk asks what on earth I am going to do with five cases of such a random drink, so I tell him my reason for choosing sherry. He is super excited to hear I am a new cast member. He says, "I'm just a big theatre queen, but [he whispers now] I have to tell you that *Mamma Mia* is my favorite show of that type. No offense."

None taken.

Upon returning to my apartment, I run through the show in my living room. It gets a little more natural every time, but the thousands of faces out there tomorrow night will probably change that. I'm feeling a little under the weather, actually, but it's probably just nerves and adrenaline messing with my system. Cara would be a calming presence to me right now. Thank God she arrives tomorrow. I don't feel right when we're apart. (As if that isn't obvious by now.)

OPENING NIGHT

WARM-UP SINGING, DRESSING ROOM GIFTS, & CHILDHOOD ODORS

June 16th, 2009

Time ticks away. The sun is bright and pierces through my window. It's difficult to sleep. There's no need to dream anymore.

8:30 a.m.— The alarm buzzes and I rise this morning to a day that I have been thinking about since the fifth grade. It has been a long journey, an exhausting journey, and sometimes a sad journey. But today, I am exhilarated. Today, I open in a leading role in a mega Broadway musical, and my wife and stepdaughter will be here to see it. I am feeling very grateful.

9:45 a.m.—After an early-morning run-through in my apartment, I get cleaned up and ready for the girls' arrival. I am so incredibly happy to see them pull up in the cab; I have spent no more than two days with them in the past six weeks. After five minutes, I feel calmer than I have in days. Rachel loves the indoor goldfish pond, as I expected, and Cara loves the size and cleanliness of our temporary digs. She makes fun of me for not having any food (coffee and cereal is all I need) and I give her directions to the theatre, as she and Rachel will be traveling without me.

12:00 p.m.—I have to leave the girls to go to my "warm-up" rehearsals. Because the opening speeches have been such a challenge for me along the way, Shelley thinks it smart to visit these speeches today in the rehearsal room, before doing them in front of an audience. This is a good rehearsal to have. It psyches me up. Shelley gives me no notes whatsoever, she just allows me to go through everything one time to get it all fresh in my brain.

3:00 p.m.—The three other Seasons come in so we can sing together. Although "Cry For Me" will probably always sound incredible to me onstage because we stand so close together while singing it, I have been told that the hundreds of bodies absorbing sound will make it hard to hear each other during many of the other songs. Singing together as a warm-up, therefore, is good for both the muscle memory and the emotional contentment...we are a vocal group, we are together, we are individuals that sing as one. That's powerful stuff. The guys sound awesome and I am a bit overcome, just like I was the first time I sang with the tour guys.

4:00 p.m.—After these rehearsals, I find myself getting really wound up. I go to my dressing room and begin running lines by myself as I decorate the room and calm myself. I have received many gifts already: a gorgeous pocket watch from my parents, flowers from my agent (with the word "finally" in the note), a large basket of dressing room goodies from Cara (a tradition she started the year we met), a picture from Rachel, and gift certificates, cards, *Jersey Boys* shot glasses, wine, and scotch from my castmates (drunks, all of them). All of this is overwhelming, just like opening nights I have dreamed about. I just wish I wasn't so nervous. I can't even read one of my cards without it quivering in my hands.

6:00 p.m.—I have a little butterfly making an appearance in my stomach.

6:03 p.m.—The butterfly flits around, tickling the inside of me so I get a bit queasy.

6:05 p.m.—The butterfly is joined by his friend.

6:17 p.m.—The butterflies are attacked by a fluttering mob from the other side of town.

6:26 p.m.—The defending butterflies sprout razor-sharp wings.

6:30 p.m.—The gang from across the tracks pull their knives, hacking away at the defenders and destroying the lining of my stomach in the process.

6:40 p.m.—The butterflies leave the scene, but announce that they will return during my first song.

7:00 p.m.—I strap on the microphone pack, grease up my hair, and pencil in my eyebrows (to match my hair color). While there is usually not a make-up department at a theatre, there is most definitely a hair room that handles all the wigs and any real hair that an actor can't handle on their own. I had a ton of practice with hair gel in high school, so I feel confident in my ability to handle the styling on my own.

7:20 p.m.—I put on my first suit. I look good.

7:30 p.m.—"Ladies and gentlemen, this is your half-hour call." I am dressed far too early.

7:45 p.m.—"Ladies and gentlemen, this is your fifteen-minute call." I drink far too much Gatorade.

7:55 p.m.—"Ladies and gentlemen, this is your five-minute call." I attempt to empty my bladder with less than complete success. I know that my low-waisted pants will probably pop open later in the show, showing the audience that Tommy has a good time onstage and off.

8:00 p.m.—"Places, please. This is your places call." I walk by five or six cast members on my way to my place in the dark. Each of them wishes me well. I step behind the chain-link fence and a black curtain that will rise just moments from now, revealing me to the audience and the audience to me. I hold on to the chain-link fence, nod to the two guys standing next to me, and try to keep my hands from shaking.

8:02 p.m.—The piano begins. It is loud. The drums kick in. They are louder. The curtain rises. And there are almost two thousand people out there staring at me.

8:03 p.m.—I slide and snap my way from my position in semi-darkness to the very center of the stage. I am blinded by the spotlight as I start to sing, but I know the audience can see me now because they are cheering. They are screaming for my entrance. (So what if it is my wife who is spurring them on.)

8:04 p.m.—I begin speaking. I cannot see the two thousand people anymore, but I sense that they are there. I probably wait too long for their reactions. I hold for laughs that aren't quite coming. Because of the blinding light, I truly fear that I may step off the front of the stage and land in the lap of one of the students who bought twenty-dollar rush tickets.

8:20 p.m.—I exit the stage for the first time. I have thirty seconds to switch guitars and realize what I've just done. So what have I done? I've delivered sixteen minutes of speeches, sung three songs, and set this big-ass show into motion.

Damn! This is unbelievable!

Damn, I am sweaty!

9:20 p.m.—Intermission. I get a number of congratulations from the cast as I make my way to my dressing room. I have been relatively calm. The butterflies

133

never came back. Although Cara will tell me later that she could see my hands shaking, I didn't actually feel nervous and I was able to get through the scenes without too much of a frantic energy.

My immediate reflections? "Cry For Me" felt like a relief to bring all the guys together, know that my narration section of the show was complete, and that I could finally settle into scenes where I speak to other actors instead of to the audience.

"Sherry" was rocking; the full band kicks in and it felt great to see all the other guys in the trademark red jackets. "Sherry" just feels cool and laid back, which made it even more fun than "Walk Like A Man," which is the big applause number. The arrangements are solid, the harmonies feel like they sneak in, and the choreography when done all together feels like it is beckoning the audience to watch, not ever attacking them with moves that are too bold. I really enjoyed doing "Sherry" today.

Quinn VanAntwerp, Daniel Robert Sullivan, Jeff Madden, Michael Lomenda

©Joan Marcus

And "Dawn!" Man, this song doesn't feel like it looks. Watching from the audience, this song was always the most visually stunning. Being in the song does not feel visually stunning but, because it was only days ago that I watched the number from the audience, I can remember how good it looks, and it was thrilling to be a part of the spectacle even if I couldn't see the special effects. I wonder whose idea it was to put in the section where the Seasons face upstage and the audience, with bright lights shining in their faces, gets a look at what it feels like to be up onstage with the band? I know that *Phantom of the Opera* has a similar scene, and that Des McAnuff had a smaller version in his production of *The Who's Tommy*, but never has the effect been done as completely as it is in "Dawn".

9:35 p.m.—"Ladies and gentlemen, places for the top of Act Two. Places, please." I walk to my place up the stairs at the top of the set. I am ready to have some real fun now. Act Two has far less for me to do, so I am looking forward to really being in the moment. Michael Lomenda, playing Nick Massi and standing right next to me, whispers to me, "You're doing great, man." I don't care if he is just being nice, I am so glad to have his (genuine or not) approval.

10:00 p.m.—We finish the Sit-Down scene and I have a fifteen-minute break in my dressing room before going back onstage. The scene was intense. Every actor brought their "A" game and was truly committed. During my break I change into a new suit, fix my hair, and go out for a chocolate shake at Dairy Queen. (Just kidding!)

10:20 p.m.—We rise from beneath the stage on a lift that presents us, the Four Seasons, to the audience one last time. We sing "Rag Doll" as we come up, and I catch the eye of a woman in about the thirteenth row who looks awestruck. If I could talk to her, I would tell her that I too am awestruck.

10:35 p.m.—We sing "Who Loves You," the finale of the show, and the full ensemble and band (even the horn section) joins us onstage. I am at the front of the group, but I can see our reflection off some glass at the very back of the theatre and I really can't believe it is me that I am seeing. This is what I've been dreaming about, right here. The lights are flashing, I am singing at the top of my lungs, the horns are blaring, and the four of us guys come together at the center of the stage. We sing one final note and raise our arms into the air. The drums crash. The lights black out, except for one that lingers on we four for one extra, magical moment. The show is over, and my dream has become a reality.

135

The audience roars.

I am sweating again.

It is dark.

I sense the audience getting up out of their seats for the ovation, cheering louder than I've ever heard. My ears are ringing. People are standing.

They are so loud.

It is very dark.

And then I realize that I am the only one left onstage in the darkness because I was supposed to exit when the lights went out.

Afterwards, the three other Seasons take me aside for a private toast. Then, Cara and Rachel join me backstage for many hugs. (Cara tells me she is proud of me. What more do I need?) And finally, the entire cast gathers in the green room for a communal toast. When asked to speak, I can only say that, "I promise it will be better tomorrow, but tonight was something I have been dreaming about for a long, long time."

I am not crying, as I expected I might. I am not laughing and high-fiving, either. I am relatively calm. Why am I not overcome with emotion? Is it because there is still work to be done?

I am so happy to be here, to have achieved something that has been my one goal (the only goal I have consistently worked towards) since grammar school. Were I to have known ten years ago that I would be opening in this kind of role in this kind of show, I would have guessed that tonight would be, well, a freak-out night. Maybe a night with happy tears. Maybe a night where I run through the streets and scream to the moon, "I did it!" But that is not how I feel tonight. Instead, I feel calmly blessed. I have worked very hard to be here, and I feel the weight of that work on my shoulders tonight. And because this kind of work has been my career for all these years, I am well aware that tonight is just another rung on the ladder and I have a lot of work to do tomorrow.

I feel calmly blessed that I have a supportive family with me here tonight, that Cara and her children supported me taking this job so far away from our daily lives.

I feel calmly blessed that my parents and brother traveled all over the country for many of my adult years to see me perform, telling me the whole time that my dream was not far-fetched, that I could make it big if I kept on.

I feel calmly blessed that I was born into a town and sent to schools that said, "Yes, you can do this," "Yes, we can help you," and "Yes, you should chase your dream."

I feel calmly blessed that, after my father passed away when I was six, my mother vowed that the purpose of her life now was to make things better for her sons, to give them every opportunity to do what made them happy ("as long as it's honest," she'd say).

I feel calmly blessed that, while I often feel lonely, I have never, ever been alone. I could not have made it here alone.

The lobby bar remains open after the show, and we are all invited out there to socialize and celebrate. The Canadian producer of *Jersey Boys*, Aubrey Dan, comes over to meet my wife and daughter. Aubrey is a gazillionaire businessman and philanthropist with a love for theatre that may even surpass my own. Having a conversation with him is a privilege, and my lovely Rachel acknowledges that privilege by passing gas the entire time he is in our circle. And that is my night in the theatre.

June 17th, 2009

There is a theatre legend of a grand dame who arrived with gusto for a matinee, only to find her cast looking tired and glum. When asked why she was looking so alive, the grand actress proclaimed, "Because I get to do it twice today!"

Today is Wednesday. And that means I get to do it twice today, too.

For the matinee (although I am having trouble remembering specifics from the performance because it went by in such a flurry and is sort of jumbled in my mind with last night's performance) I did well, markedly better than last night. The crowd was right with us, and I was relaxed, in the moment, and singing as well as I am able to.

137

This picture was taken in the theatre lobby directly following my first performance. Michael Lomenda, me, Jeff Madden, Quinn VanAntwerp.

The evening show is also relaxed. Maybe too relaxed. During one of my opening speeches I get some kind of phlegm caught in my throat and my lines begin sounding like a talking frog. I know I have to sing "Earth Angel" in just a few moments, so I stop talking, cough (which is never a good sound when blasted into a microphone), give a little smirk, and continue on. I am not exactly sure why the phlegm built up, but I do have a theory: I forgot to swallow. I have so many lines at the top of the show that I think I just forgot to swallow in my efforts to get them all out. I will have to work on this basic human function over the next week.

Say line.

Breathe.

Swallow.

Say line.

Swallow.

Breathe.

Sing.

Swallow.

Sing again.

With three performances under my belt, I have no more adrenaline pumping through my veins, and that leaves my lungs aching for air, my knee cramping, and my neck as stiff as if I were wearing a brace. I'm going to curl up next to Cara now and sleep for the next ten to fifteen years.

June 18th, 2009

Cara, Rachel, and I have breakfast today at a little coffee shop that looks out onto a busy Toronto street. Rachel is now, officially, a well-traveled little girl. Cara is now, officially, the most supportive wife in the world. And I am now, officially, working my dream job—but in the wrong city. Cara and Rachel leave for the airport after breakfast, and I am alone again.

I travel up to the theatre for rehearsal, but this time the rehearsal is not my own. Because of Lindsay's medical leave of absence, a new actress has been hired to play Francine. Alison Smyth has been rehearsing (largely on her own, as I did) for the past ten days or so, and today's rehearsal is all about working her into the show. I am feeling a little down to be without my family again, so I am glad not to be the "new guy" for this rehearsal. I prefer to be left alone for a bit.

The evening's show is full of misadventures. Michael has a bit of phlegm during one of his speeches (swallow, Michael, swallow!) and has to stop to cough. After coughing, he says, "Excuse me," and continues on with his line, "Frankie and Lorraine were...great. Frankie was...awesome." Awesome? "Awesome" is not a word used in the 1960s with any regularity, and is certainly not a word used in *Jersey Boys* at all, so we find it necessary to poke fun at this otherwise impenetrable actor for the rest of the night.

But there is more! During the Sit-Down scene, the actor playing Norm says "Las Vegas" instead of "Nevada" in one of his lines; a very small mistake, but enough to throw off the rhythm. Frankie seems to forget his next line, and Gyp DeCarlo comes in with, "Best I could do!" Then, Frankie remembers his line, so Gyp comes in again with, "Best I could do!" Gyp is a broken record, "Best I could do!" Though everyone remains serious and in the moment, it lightens the mood of a very stressful week for us all.

I am quite sure that having a new lead actor in such a tightly established show is hard on everyone here. While it is a dream come true for me, it has made a lot more work for everyone else. And the other lead guys in the show have lost a good friend in Jeremy. I am forever the new guy. And I am the new guy who is completely by himself. Though, Cara, Rachel, and Mark will be up here in a couple weeks, I have been away from their daily lives since April. This is not something I can do forever. And I am ok with that.

No matter what I do with the rest of my life, I will always be able to say that I played a lead role in a blockbuster Broadway musical.

And so, I have two final details to record before I close my journal and begin going to work every day at that glorious place. First, the Toronto Company of *Jersey Boys* has a capacity audience tonight, having sold out the entire theatre for the first time in the building's sixteen-year history. Second, Shelley has assured me that I have done a sufficiently good job, good enough that I am in absolutely no danger of being fired.

So I'm sticking around. For now. This is going to be a wild ride.

ACT III

RUNNING THE SHOW

ENTOURAGE, BATHROOM RENOVATIONS, & COWBOYS

11th Show

It's one of those thick and muggy summer nights, the kind of night that keeps people milling about the theatre grounds long after the show has finished. We had another sold-out crowd and almost two thousand people just spilled onto the streets of Toronto, moving slowly as they hit the wall of hot air outside. They are moving so slowly, in fact, that I run off stage after my bow, change out of my costume, and take a shower all before the last few audience members leave the building. Cara and Rachel, both finally in Toronto for the entire summer, meet me in my dressing room after the show and we get ready to leave.

"Daniel?" Rachel tugs at my shirt as we begin to walk down the hallway. "Daniel?"

"Yes, Rach?"

"Come here." She pulls me down to her seven-year-old height and whispers in my ear. "Can you tell them I'm your daughter?" She leaves out the "step" and has made the word just daughter.

"Tell who that you're my daughter?"

"The people outside." We haven't been outside yet.

"What people are you talking about?"

"The people who want to take pictures with you."

And now I understand. Rachel figured out there is a bit of mini-celebrity status in coming out the stage door of a show like *Jersey Boys*; there are always people out there waiting for an autograph, a picture, or a few words. The way my wife puts it, it is their way of "prolonging the experience; making the good feelings last longer." And on hot summer nights, as Rachel also figured out, there are bound to be a lot of people waiting out there.

Rachel wants to be my entourage. While it is possible that she has preemptively asked me to eliminate the "step" in her introduction because of some deep psychological distaste for the word, I'm pretty sure her request is just a way of being a little closer to mini-celebrity status herself. She wants to be cool. And don't we all?

So we exit the theatre and sure enough there are:

- large groups of pre-teen girls who squeal (even if they are squealing at the younger, cuter actor exiting behind me),
- middle-aged women out for a night on the town who have clearly had some (and some more) wine,
- theatre students who look like they could be in the cast of Glee (and probably will be someday),
- and even a few husband-wife pairs in which the husband looks just as enthusiastic as the wife.

I stop at the group nearest the stage door to thank them for coming and sign their programs when they request. But I take too long. It has been about twenty seconds and I have not yet introduced Rachel as my daughter like she requested. She is feeling left out. She wants to be noticed, too. And so Rachel begins pulling on my shirt again, this time speaking at the top of her voice, "Daddy! Daaaadddy!"

She has never called me that. And she probably never will again. But it feels pretty good to hear it right now.

15th Show

Performing in a big musical is a job. Let us make no mistake about that. It is a joyous, creative, and thrilling job, but a job nonetheless.

It is a job that needs to be kept in order to pay the bills.

It is a job represented by a union with definite rules and regulations that must be followed. Late for work three times? I can be charged. Ignore a piece of direction I have been given? I can be charged. Exit stage left instead of stage right just because I feel like it? I can be charged. (And something will probably hit me in the head.)

It is a job that absolutely requires an actor's presence. Yes, I have an understudy. Usually I have two. But what if one of them is sick? That leaves only two of us. And train/highway delays happen with regularity. Family emergencies happen, too. But one of us needs to be here or the show will have to be cancelled and two thousand people will be sent home. Has this ever happened? Hmm. Not that I've heard of. That's because in the professional world of theatre, it is an actor's job to be present and ready to perform no matter what. Actors who drive the highway leave an hour early, just in case. Actors who take the train still make sure to have money for a cab, just in case. And actors who have family emergencies sometimes have to ignore that family emergency. That's just the way it is.

Performing in a big musical is also a job that needs to be improved and tweaked as time goes by. Notes are given constantly, and it is part of my job to adjust my performance accordingly. In my first weeks running *Jersey Boys*, the cumulative amount of notes I am receiving from the dance captain, fight captain, production stage manager, and musical director is overwhelming. By week two, I have fourteen handwritten pages of things I need to fix. One particularly piercing example comes right before a Saturday matinee.

"Dan?" There is a knock on my dressing room door. It is our production stage manager. "You have a minute?"

"Sure!" I yell as I put down my gallon jug of hair gel and open the door.

"Listen," she says quietly, "I don't really know how to say this, so I'm just going to come right out with it. Some of the other guys are feeling disconnected from you onstage, like they don't feel they understand what is going on during certain scenes with you."

Well, ok. (I'm a little hurt now.) Do you think that could be because I only rehearsed with them twice before opening? (I'm a little bitter now.) Do you think that could be because we have never had a chance to actually work on the scenes together? (I'm a little angry now.) It is great that we all want honesty in our scene work, but the way to get that honesty is to rehearse, not to give me notes that the other guys don't feel connected to what I'm doing. (I'm a lot angry now.)

But, "Ok, thanks for the note," is all I can actually say out loud.

I am working very hard to create the best performance I am capable of doing, and it hurts very much to get this kind of note about my scene work, especially when I have always felt scene work is my strong point. The guitar playing, dancing, and singing are all things I have worked to death on so that I am up to par, but they have never been my strongest selling points. But the scene work... I'm not naturally tough, of course, but I can act these scenes. This note I got feels contrary to what I believe about myself. I cannot be acting badly; it has to be that I am just acting differently from what they're used to. It has to be.

21st Show

Enough time passes that I feel comfortable enough in Tommy DeVito's skin to let my parents come see the show. The past few weeks have tortured my mother like a little kid who missed the party because she is sent to time-out. My mom wanted to be here on my opening night, but I wouldn't let her. I wanted to get better first.

My parents saw me rise through the ranks. They watched when I sang a solo for the first time in *The Fantasticks* in 10th grade. They attended my first big leading role in a regional theatre, driving all the way to Virginia to see it. They watched me on the big screen when I sang in Spielberg's *Amistad*, a five-second appearance that they talked about for five years after. And they are here at *Jersey Boys* for today's matinee.

My stepfather is proud of me. He worked extremely hard for his own position in life, and appreciates the idea of setting your mind to a career goal and sticking to it. He appreciates my struggle almost more than my accomplishment. (Although he appreciates my accomplishment too, as proven by his frequent visits to the *Jersey Boys Blog*.) He gives me a huge hug after the performance and smiles a larger smile than I've seen on him in a long time.

My mother is proud of me too. And crying. I hope she thinks she has done a good job with me, because she has. She never let me forget about my dream. She would ask, "Are you sure this day job is going to give you time to audition?" Not many parents of small-time actors would say something like that.

And in a clear demonstration of their personality, my parents do not rush to me at the stage door. They wait behind the crowd because they don't want to interfere with any fans waiting to have programs signed or pictures taken. I have to pull them in to me to receive their hugs and tears. They still don't seem to realize that theirs is the approval I seek, because they are the ones who have been with me every step of the way.

They buy another pair of tickets for tonight's show. And another pair for tomorrow's show. And I make them ask me to autograph their programs, just for kicks.

33rd Show

A month goes by. We perform the show eight times every week, and living in the role for so many hours a day lets me flesh it out, adding nuances and becoming more and more truthful with my portrayal. The creative team begins visiting our company. Director Des McAnuff, Production Supervisor Richard Hester, Associate Director West Hyler, Music Supervisor Ron Melrose, Choreographer Sergio Trujillo, Associate Choreographer Danny Austin, and many others with slightly lower carvings on the totem pole attend performances. Their response to my work can truly make or break my career. Being fired would be embarrassing and tough to explain to future casting directors, and being lauded could offer me a long future with *Jersey Boys* or any of the other hits these artists work with each season. So I try to bribe them all.

When bribery doesn't work (I have nothing really to offer except my old baseball cards, but I'm saving them until retirement), I have to live with the creative team's genuine response. And their response means everything.

From one: "You were very good."

From another: "You are doing a truly great job."

From my favorite: "Yours was one of the most enjoyable performances I've seen. Ever."

And now I love my job even more. With these compliments come pages and pages of new notes, but the notes are encouraging and offer me clear direction on where to go. I'm not perfect, but I have found a joy in performing this material that seems to be showing through. Joy is infectious. And it seems to have infected those in charge.

41st Show

The New York Times once said I have the "seductive magnetism of a snake-oil salesman." I have always loved that quote. (Cara says the same thing about me when I unbutton my shirt further than usual. Ok, no she doesn't.)

I will receive no such endorsement from Canadian publications, for I am "merely" a replacement actor and there have been no major reviews of my work in this show. There is, however, plenty of less official commentary finding its way to me:

On YouTube: "Daniel Robert Sullivan has been absolutely phenomenal and brings even more of an edge to and a different take on the character. His quirky facial expressions and nuances are worth seeing alone." Written by silver6342.

On a local entertainment site: "Daniel Robert Sullivan is pure magic as Tommy DeVito. Truly, he is New Jersey incarnate in this role, with an incredible accent and this unmistakably American command of not only himself, but of the three other boys...It is fascinating to watch this character evolve and how brilliantly Sullivan is able to convey such subtlety, and even traces of vulnerability, in a character with such a larger than life intensity that is so reliant on a reputation for toughness to survive." Written by Amanda Campbell.

In fan mail: "You are sexy and awesome." Written by Candace.

On the *Jersey Boys* Fan Forum: "Daniel was fantastic!" Written by my Aunt Jude.

And on some blog written by a guy I've never heard of: "If I had to pick a weakest link in the show, it would definitely be Daniel Robert Sullivan."

This is why some actors don't read reviews. Even though the professional response I've received is positive, the presence of this one blog comment in my Google Alert this morning has ruined my confidence for the day. I don't need to be the best, but I certainly don't want to be the worst!

Perhaps I should take refuge in one of my favorite theatre stories: Harvey Fierstein was performing in the smash-hit play *Torch Song Trilogy*, a play he also authored, when Ethel Merman came to visit him backstage. When Harvey asked her what she thought of the play, Ms. Merman replied, "I thought it was a piece of shit, but the rest of the audience laughed and cried, so what the fuck do I know?"

There's always going to be someone who doesn't like the way you do it.

49th Show

I enjoy a life of routine. I always arrive at the theatre one hour before curtain. I sign in, say hello to the stage management office, and briefly check in with any cast members that already arrived. I go to my dressing room and fill out a status board that I placed outside the door: "Dan Sullivan is...having a bad hair day." "Dan Sullivan is...feeling bloated." "Dan Sullivan is...wondering which one of you placed the five-foot high picture of Frankie Valli in his bathroom." This is my way of reaching out to those cast members that I don't see in the pre-show hubbub, and usually inspires someone to use the pen I provide to write some snarky comment in response. (At my expense, of course. Always at my expense.)

I arrange my small props: a deck of cards, a necklace, guitar picks. I do some pull-ups on my costume rack. (If anybody from the wardrobe department reads this, they are definitely going to stop me from doing pull-ups on my costume rack.) By a half-hour before the show, I am in the shower and singing. I leave my hair a little wet, put on my special black underwear (so colored in case I happen to leave my fly unzipped someday), strap on my microphone rig, and slick my hair back. I put on my first suit, smear on some Covergirl foundation, pencil in my eyebrows, and brush my teeth. This last part makes me feel fresh and ready to go, and helps me feel less disgusting when I have to kiss two of the actresses later in the show.

All of these steps are done alone. I leave my dressing room door open whenever I am not doing embarrassing things (like trying to locate a six-pack underneath my soft belly), but most people are busy with their own routines and have no time for visits.

So I bring in a television and a Wii. And now they have time for visits. Intermission is game time.

"Power serve!" I am sweating already.

"Coming back atcha...There ya go!" Michael Lomenda is sweating even more. (But still not quite as much as he does when onstage.)

"Ooo, backhand coming...Score!" I am winning.

"Ok. Serve it up again."

"Forehand and score!"

"Damn. Game point for you?" Michael seems sad as he says this.

"Yup. Here it comes...Serve and score! Game, set, and match!" I am gloating. "I killed you, man! Easiest game ever! You want a rematch?"

"No. I'll just go back to my room and get ready for Act Two." (Note: The above conversation is entirely fictional. Michael is an unbelievable Wii tennis player and I have not beaten him a single time. But I figure that publishing an account of me winning will make me feel better about not accomplishing the task in real life.)

My dressing room is also full of *Scientific American* and *Skeptic* magazines, books by A.J. Jacobs and Michael Lewis, DVDs of Broadway shows, a dart board, an iPod player, and a five-foot high Scooby-Doo I rescued from the building next door's dumpster and hung from my ceiling. I have wireless internet access, a comfy blue couch, and a bathroom with a shower. And a cleaning service. If this was New York, my dressing room could be a $1600 per month studio apartment. Toronto's *Eye Weekly* newspaper actually did a feature on it. (Yes. I haven't received any press in the newspapers around here, but my dressing room has.)

53rd Show

After many weeks, the show still exhausts and injures me. We perform at night from Tuesday to Saturday, and in the afternoons on Wednesday, Saturday, and Sunday; with Monday being our only day off. This is a very typical Broadway schedule, and grueling enough to force me to be conscious of resting my body and voice when I am not onstage.

Often, I will find a large cut on my arm or a serious pain in my foot and not know the cause until the next performance. I'll do a move during the show and say, "Ouch! That's how I did that to myself!" My knees are especially injury-prone, for I run up and down two hundred and fifty-two stairs per show. That's over two thousand stairs per week. Running around the stage like that is dangerous, as one of the other *Jersey Boys* can tell you. Quinn VanAntwerp was in his third month of doing the show as Bob, and wailing with that powerful voice I first heard so long ago. One night, he was given new shoes to wear. Sounds nice, right? New shoes are comfortable, and the wardrobe department spends a lot of time breaking them in and re-rubbering the soles so they have more traction. However, the rubber used on these shoes doesn't provide great traction on the metal bridge section of the set. But nobody knew that yet.

Remember, the metal bridge is ten feet in the air. Quinn sang the first verse of "Oh, What A Night," then ran across the bridge to sing the second verse a little further upstage. In the space between the two verses (which is exactly 3.55 seconds), he slid under the safety railing and halfway off the side of the bridge, broke his left hand, caught himself with his right hand, pulled himself back up again with that right hand, and sang the second verse without missing a beat.

That, my friends, is simply unbelievable. But totally true. During Quinn's next quick-change, our dresser Andy had to help cover the blood that was pouring out of a large gash in Quinn's side. And Bob Gaudio played piano with a cast on his hand for the next month. (Because this story is so manly and cool, I'm going to leave out the part about how long and loudly Quinn screamed when Andy cleaned the wound with alcohol during intermission. Quinn wouldn't like it if I published how long and loudly he screamed. Because it was quite long. And quite loud.)

61st Show

The *Jersey Boys* are asked to do a lot of special events and appearances, some for charity and some for publicity. When approved by all parties, we are allowed (and often required) to perform special medleys of *Jersey Boys* songs. Recall that we are contractually forbidden from performing these songs anywhere on our own, but exceptions are made for charity and publicity events, if approved by the Canadian public relations firm, the New York public relations firm, the Canadian producers, the New York producers, stage management, company management, Bob Gaudio, and Frankie Valli. (As you can guess, there are a lot of conference calls in the *Jersey Boys* world.)

For charity, we have raised hundreds of thousands of dollars in the lobby through the generosity of our audiences; whenever a "cause" comes up, I am surprised at the amount of people who will drop $20 bills into our buckets. For publicity, we have appeared on countless news programs, commercials, and even *Entertainment Tonight*, teaching one of the hosts our signature moves. We have performed at large festivals, each one requiring us to have a police escort. That's right. A police escort! Rachel was with me for the first of these and asked, "What do the police need to protect us from?"

I was wondering the same thing, Rachel.

A police escort actually seems a bit silly, doesn't it? No real need for these escorts, I think to myself as we perform at another large outdoor event. It's cool, but unnecessary. It's not like we're going to be mobbed by thousands of screaming...

Wait. There are a lot of people at this event today. Thousands, actually. And they are screaming very loudly and pushing quite hard to get up to the front of the stage. Wow! This feels great. I'm like a rock star! I guess this is why we have these police escorts, because young girls do go crazy when they see... (It is about here I realize the Jonas Brothers are behind us waiting to take the stage. And that explains everything.)

62nd Show

OMG. We totally opened for the Jonas Brothers yesterday.

70th Show

It is August, and today marks the one-year anniversary of *Jersey Boys* in Toronto. It isn't the one-year anniversary for me, of course, but I do get to take part in the festivities and publicity. The greatest part? Bob Gaudio, the real Bob Gaudio, comes to see the show and invites us to lunch.

We performed at this outdoor fundraiser, and the Jonas Brothers appeared after us!
©Daniel Robert Sullivan

He and his wife, Judy Parker, are classy and kind. Their fame and fortune has not removed their graciousness. (And Bob orders the same risotto special that I do, making me feel like I've made a proper choice.)

We are told a great story: "December 1963 (Oh, What A Night)" is one of the band's greatest hits, but it may not have made it were it not for Judy's input. Apparently, this song was written by Bob with a lyric celebrating the repeal of prohibition. Bob was not entirely happy with the lyric, but on the eve of the recording session he had yet to come up with a better idea. The historical narrative lyric would have to do. ("Late December, back in thirty-three...")

At 3:00 a.m., Judy Parker rises from bed with an inspiration. She goes to the living room and writes a new lyric for Bob's melody, a lyric that alludes to a boy's first sexual encounter. The following morning, the band records this lyric and the song rises to No. 1 on the charts in March, 1976.

Behind every great man, there is a great woman...or at least a great lyricist.

Hanging out with the real Bob Gaudio.

©Daniel Robert Sullivan

88th Show

And speaking of great women, it is time for my two to go home. Cara begins a new season helping to create wigs for *Saturday Night Live*, and Rachel starts school. Mark returns from his first job at the summer camp in a few days, and I am left in Toronto. Alone again.

I predict that Rachel will be going through a bit of *Jersey Boys* withdrawal. She became quite obsessed with the show in these past months. We initially debated whether or not to let her see it because of the bad language, but eventually decided that the show was too much a part of our lives not to let her experience it. We talked about the swear words and how she should not repeat them. We told her I am playing a "bad guy," and that's the only reason I speak this way. So what did she do? She began repeating her favorite line in the show, a line that has no swear words at all: "I want you inside me."

How do we explain that one? Our solution was to tell her that some of the lines in the show are adult jokes, and that she should not repeat those either. She seemed to understand and we didn't hear her say anything undesirable again.

Until today.

154

Rachel's first day of school. She attends a Catholic school and there is one (only one) nun on staff. Rachel loves Sister Margie. So much so that she wants to tell her all about her summer in Toronto. But first Rachel wants to tell a joke that Sister Margie is bound to appreciate because it is an "adult joke." So Rachel pulls Sister Margie down to her knees and whispers in her ear, "I want you inside me." And Rachel laughs and laughs and laughs. We have to explain that one very carefully to Sister Margie.

104th Show

I take the bus home to New York on this Sunday night in September. I leave Toronto at 7:30 p.m. and arrive in Manhattan at 6:00 a.m. the following morning. After arriving back at our apartment for the first time since rehearsing the show, I crawl into bed next to my beautiful sleeping wife who I have not seen in two weeks. We just have one day together before I fly back to Toronto at 11:00 a.m. tomorrow.

We quickly realize that this is not enough time together.

"Cara, I can't go two weeks without being home with you. We need to do something different."

"I know. Screw the budget. Let's just get you tickets to come home every week."

So I begin coming home every week, taking the bus on Sunday and flying back on Tuesday. The bus trip saves us money.

After some time of this Cara says, "Daniel, I love that you are willing to take the bus to come home to us, but seeing you only on Monday is not enough."

"I know. But we don't really have extra money for me to fly both ways. The bus is cheap!"

"So I say again, screw the budget."

She's right. Screw the budget. I buy plane tickets for every Sunday night through Tuesday afternoon for the rest of my contract year. We cannot put money into our savings account this way, but we are happier. Much happier.

Every Sunday afternoon at 4:35 p.m. I take my final bow. I run into my dressing room, jump in the shower, and am out of the building by 4:45. I take the subway and then a cab to the airport (this transportation combination is the quickest). I whip through security like George Clooney in *Up in the Air*. I fly, landing in Newark, New Jersey by 7:30. I bound up three flights of stairs to be the first in line at customs, run through the airport (taking a shortcut that I refuse to put in print for fear it will be closed off) to catch the next train to Manhattan, and am in my apartment by 8:45 p.m., where I enjoy Sunday night dinner with my family. And I've come to realize that it is well worth screwing our budget to have that dinner.

149th Show

More weeks go by. I'm settled into the physical requirements of the show and my body hurts a lot less (although I still slice my arm on guitar strings once in a while). I receive a tremendous amount of support from family and friends; it seems like every weekend a different cousin drives ten hours to see the show, only to return home the following day. And I feel more and more comfortable onstage.

Being in front of almost two thousand people is not as nerve-wracking as one might think. While the beginning of the show will always get my adrenaline pumping, once we settle into the story, I feel quite calm. So calm, in fact, that I have recently found myself multi-tasking.

I sing "Sherry" and I think about when the next sale at Porter Airlines will come up. I sing "Big Girls Don't Cry" and consider what to have for dinner, a burger or pasta. I sing "Walk Like A Man" and realize I have run out of Fruit Loops in my dressing room. (Fruit Loops are great for immediate energy when my blood sugar gets low, and they are high in fiber.) (That last sentence is my way of justifying the unhealthy cereal I am completely addicted to.)

My body remembers what to do. If I ever fear for a second that the words or moves will not come out, I need simply abandon active thought and let my body react; the correct lines and moves will happen. Muscle memory seems to be a very real phenomenon, so forgetting lines becomes the least of our troubles. Some of our recent plights:

156

- The Problem: The elevator lift carrying many of the microphones and set pieces breaks during my first song, leaving us without a way to move things on and off the stage.

- The Solution: The production stage manager makes an announcement to all the swings hanging out in their dressing rooms to put on a costume and begin carrying things on and off as needed. (A swing is often told to play a role at the last minute, but I can't recall another time when all the swings were called upon to help out at the same time.)

- The Problem: The onstage drummer becomes terribly nauseous right before the show, and cannot find a substitute because it is so last minute. (Actor understudies at *Jersey Boys* must be present at the theatre; not so with musician subs.)

- The Solution: A bucket is placed at his feet "just in case." And he uses it. Many times. And yet he never misses a beat! (Pun intended.)

- The Problem: An actor misses a cue and doesn't show up for one of his scenes, a scene that reveals the group's new name to be the Four Seasons. (An important plot point, don't you think?)

- The Solution: Two other actors find a way to segue into the next scene (I am absolutely no help in this), leaving the show a few minutes shorter and us hoping the audience just catches on to the fact that we have a new name.

- The Problem: After the twentieth expletive uttered in Act Two of the show, an audience member yells out, "Stop swearing!" He has already listened to about fifty such words up to this point.

- The Solution: We make fun of him backstage.

160th Show

It's official. Tommy DeVito has infiltrated Daniel Robert Sullivan. Not only am I swearing a lot more, but I am refusing to take any shit from anyone. Period. (Yeah, that's right, I said "shit.")

After receiving an unjustified parking ticket here in my own building, I respectfully complain six times to ever-higher officials in the building management, but am given the runaround each and every time. Finally, I begin yelling. A lot.

I harass them. I try to use my neighborhood mini-celebrity status. I write a seven-page letter to the Board of Directors, complete with full-color pictures and diagrams. I file in small claims court. I even submit my name to be elected to the Board of Directors so I can fight from the inside. Tommy DeVito never gives up.

And I win.

I arrive home today to find a reimbursement check from the building management. Surely the best thirty-five dollars I've earned in a long time.

173rd Show

While letting some of Tommy's personality traits take over my own is fun, I do have to make sure I keep some of them in check. Snapping my fingers at Cara when I want something done, for example, proves to be a very bad marital technique. Yelling when I am angry is equally uncalled for, as I have to remind myself this week. I arrive home in New York on Sunday evening ready for a peaceful and relaxing day off, and a sleep in my own bed. But Cara has a surprise for me. She is excited. She is proud. She has redone our bathroom.

Now, most guys would probably think a new paint job, a shelf, and some plants would be nice, especially if the guy didn't have to lift a finger to have it all completed. But I react very differently. I am angry. Tommy DeVito wants to yell. But Daniel Robert Sullivan tries to keep him in check.

"Cara, why didn't you tell me you wanted to do this?"

"Because I wanted it to be a surprise. Why do I have to tell you?"

"What do you mean, 'why do I have to tell you?'" (Anger is bubbling inside me. Tommy DeVito is about to emerge.)

"Why do I have to tell you when I want to redo the bathroom?"

"You have to tell me because it is our bathroom, not your bathroom!" (Stop yelling, Tommy DeVito.)

"Well, you are being controlling. First, I didn't even think you'd care that much about the color of the bathroom. And second, I should be able to change it if I want to change it. You're hardly here anyway."

"I'm here every fucking week!" (Stop swearing, Tommy DeVito.)

"Yeah, I know. And you always find something to fight about the day you get home."

Cara is right; I always find something to fight about the day I get home.

I'm going to be unfair now and use this book as a way of getting in the last word in our debate. (Note to guys: Getting in the last word by publishing a book is also not a good marital technique.) I am upset not because of the bathroom change itself, but because I was left out of the change. Because I am hardly ever at our home, I want all the more to be included in decisions made. To relinquish my vote is to relinquish my involvement, and I want desperately to stay involved. I am angry because I was not involved today.

The bathroom looks really great, though. But don't tell Cara I said that.

205th Show

I never throw out a playbill. I have a tremendous storage case full of them dating back to 1988. My favorite part of the publicity surrounding my joining this company of *Jersey Boys* was when it was announced on Playbill.com. When I began performing this role, updated playbills were not back from the printer and so the audience received full-color cardboard inserts with my picture and bio. Michael Lomenda called these inserts "rather fancy," and I was sure I would find hundreds of them in the trash outside the theatre. When the new playbills arrived, there was no longer a use for the inserts, and last week I was allowed to take them. Three thousand photos of me.

So I went to the theatre two hours early and used them to cover the walls, ceiling, and mirrors in Michael's dressing room. Playing pranks is a theatre tradition. While most actors are professional enough to keep the pranks far from the stage itself, there is always excitement when someone gets punked.

One of our guitar players has a talking stuffed parrot that he has made speak only lines from *Jersey Boys*. But that parrot is "kidnapped" all the time. Once, the parrot sent pictures of itself on the beach in Mexico. Another time, the parrot was found hanging in a noose forty feet above the stage with a bright spotlight trained on it. The parrot even sent pictures of itself on top of the Empire State Building.

Quinn VanAntwerp's dressing room flooded a few times...in one day. So fellow castmates removed everything from his room and set him up again, not in another dressing room, but in the main hallway of our building. It "forced" him to reside in this hallway for four days.

I made a joke about a chicken once. The band heard it; it was not a good joke. But the next night there was a live chicken in my apartment when I arrived home after the show.

My chief dresser, Andy, is the one in charge of making sure every costume I wear is in perfect condition and in the right location before each show. He is also in charge of my quick-changes, which means he spends part of every day on his knees in front of me while I wear nothing but my underwear. So I began attaching signs to the front of my underwear. I wore these miniature signs through the show, revealing them to Andy when I stripped down in front of him backstage. Some recent signage: "Andy's Fan Club," "Jersey Boy," "Are You Having A Good Day?" and "Warning: Explosives Inside."

Michael plays Nick, a character who is very quiet and seemingly in control...until he explodes in a comic rage. This character mimics Michael's actual personality, making him a fun target for mischief-making. (The photos of me that now line his walls are not nearly enough of a prank.)

Michael's dressing room is next to mine; so last month I came to the theatre early, crawled up above the ceiling tiles, and rigged up a rope that I can pull from my room to cause his entire ceiling to lift, shift, and rattle. I do this only a little bit each day, just enough to drive him crazy, without making it an obvious prank. He is convinced that the rattling is mice. Or rats.

Finally, today, I gather seven cast members in my room before the show. I pull the rope harder than ever, making the ceiling actually rain plaster dust all over his room. He needs only ten seconds to figure out what's going on and charges into my room, with comic rage flaring, to the cast's applause. He's a good guy. And good guys deserve to have pranks pulled on them!

160

I'd like to think I'm a good guy, too. Maybe that's why I'm becoming convinced that the fan mail I've been receiving lately is not actually from real fans...

240th Show

Christmas Eve. We have just one show today, and it's a matinee. I'm not sure, but I think we shaved at least five minutes off the show with everyone rushing through dialogue to get home to their families. My trek home begins by trudging through the slush outside the stage door at 5:00 p.m., racing to the airport by 6:00, being delayed until 11:30, and arriving home in New York at 2:00 a.m. December 25th is a day off, and a simple and joyous one it will be. I'll have to return to Toronto to do two performances on December 26th, but the short time at home is well worth it. My parents will join us for Christmas Day, and we plan to have dinner at the kosher Second Avenue Deli. Now if that isn't a New York Christmas, I don't know what is.

267th Show

Winter is harsh in Toronto. I am lucky to live next door to the theatre, and the underground parking garage that connects the two buildings means that I have no real reason to go outside. At all. The crowds in the theatre are still huge, still thrilling. But they don't come to the stage door anymore. Too cold, I guess. We have no interaction with them, and somehow that changes this whole experience.

Perhaps my want for audience interaction stems from a selfish need for personal approval; although I would like to think of myself as above that. Their applause should be enough, right? Or perhaps my want for interaction is simply a need for basic human contact. I see no one all day long, then see my co-workers at the theatre only briefly before the show and during intermission. I'm lonely; that's all it is. The show remains the most satisfying artistic experience I've had, but it also remains the right job in the wrong city. I'm itching for home.

331st Show

It's my birthday, and Cara hasn't called me much today. We usually talk twenty times a day, so why she would be unavailable through most of today puzzles me. And truly hurts me.

Quinn invited people down to the local BBQ joint after the show for a small cowboy-themed birthday party. I didn't realize he knew I own a cowboy hat. And that I absolutely love that cowboy hat. At intermission, the cast sings for me and presents me with an ice cream cake. (That's the only kind of cake I like. How'd they know that?)

Intermission is over, and it has now been four hours since I've heard from Cara. Not cool, right? I call her, and she does not pick up. I know she is a very busy person, but I also know her schedule well enough to understand that she shouldn't be particularly busy today.

I do the beginning of Act Two and finish the Sit-Down scene by two "thugs" escorting me off stage. When we have left the stage, one of the thugs stops me. He hands me an envelope from his pocket. He's carried the envelope with him through the entire scene. I open it, and inside is a copy of a plane ticket with Cara's name on it.

I enter my dressing room knowing what to expect. There is my wife waiting for me, kicking back in a cowboy hat that matches mine. It's her first visit to Toronto since last summer.

She is the reason behind the ice cream cake. She is the reason behind the cowboy-themed party. And she is the reason that the BBQ place is covered in fifteen "Wanted" posters with my picture on them, posters that were there all day and were probably viewed by many of the folks who had dinner there before seeing the show.

I'm going to sleep well tonight. I'm "wanted" after all.

My cowboy hat. In my dressing room.
©*Daniel Robert Sullivan*

368th Show

I am often asked if I get sick of doing the same thing every day. I have done the show hundreds of times now, and I suppose it is a fair question. The answer is simple. First, I could never get sick of doing this show. And second, it is not at all the same thing every day.

To the first part of my response, *Jersey Boys* is one of the most well-crafted musicals ever written. It never fails to engage an audience, and it is full of characters that are enjoyable to play and have a fully fleshed-out journey. It's way better than *Cats*. And I love *Cats*. My new goal (here it comes) is to be in this same show in New York. That would be the perfect life for me—artistically satisfied and close to home. (I guess that would be the perfect life for anybody.) I would stay in this show in New York until they kicked me out, and even then I would be happy to play it again in some community theatre in Brooklyn. I love it that much.

To the second part of my response, the show never quite plays out the same because of the million variables that go into it. The audience can change the show, for they can energize us with their laughter or make us work harder with their silence. A different keyboard player can change the show, for a song can drive harder or softer depending on which substitute is playing. The two sound mixers can change the show, for they never set levels the exact same way as the day before. An understudy filling in for a principal actor can change the show, for the actor can have a very different take on a character (permissible as long as it is in the same ballpark). Alternate drummers, conductors, stage managers, ensemble members, and spotlight operators all impact the overall feel of the performance, and there is rarely a show with the full "regular" cast and crew. In fact, there have probably been only two or three shows this month where everyone was running their regular track. The people change, and so a show is never quite the same as the next.

371st Show

Actors in big shows like *Jersey Boys* are allowed to take a handful of vacation days, during which the actor's understudy will perform the role. I have never been in such a long run of a show before and I have not missed a show due to illness a single time in my life, so "giving up" performances to take a vacation still seems foreign to me. But it is a privilege I have earned, so I take it.

A year ago, I desperately wanted to attend the *Saturday Night Live* wrap party with my wife, but couldn't because of my rehearsals for *Jersey Boys*. I take some vacation days to be her date to this season's party, and have another brush with small-scale celebrity.

The party is held on the grounds of the Rockefeller Center Ice Skating Rink. Seven hundred people attend, many of them recognizable celebrities. We dance, we mingle, we drink, and we eat. I am alone at the bar with Lorne Michaels and all I can say is, "Hey." Then we end up in a large circle of chattering NBC employees, only a few of whom Cara knows. From across this circle comes a loud call to me, "Tommy DeVito! Didn't I see you in *Jersey Boys* in Toronto a few months ago?!"

I am used to being recognized at the Starbucks across from the theatre in Toronto. But being recognized at 3:00 a.m. in the middle of Rockefeller Center is a much cooler thing.

379th Show

The Tony Awards are coming up this Sunday, and I am obsessive about them as always. We *Jersey Boys* give an interview that will be played during the Canadian broadcast of the awards, and I have already entered five separate Tony gambling pools. (I didn't enter so many to give different guesses in each pool, I entered because I am totally confident my guesses are correct and I want to win five separate prizes.) And we find out a glorious piece of information while at work today: a two-minute video of the Toronto Company of *Jersey Boys* will be shown on a giant screen during the Tony Awards presentation at Radio City Music Hall in New York! It will not be shown on television, but will fill one of the commercial breaks for the almost six thousand people watching the Tonys in person. So, I am (sort of) performing at the Tony Awards this year. Another dream can (sort of) be checked off my list.

383rd Show

It has been more than a year now since I had my final audition for *Jersey Boys*, and the trembling hands are still with me. They are with me when I hold onto the chain-link fence for my first entrance. They are with me when I reveal the car keys to Frankie in the scene I auditioned with long ago. And they remain with me now as I try to come to terms with the decision Cara and I have to make.

"They want me to stay just a little bit longer." My agent has called with another offer from the producers to extend my contract.

165

"Are you quoting a song right now?" Cara is with me again for the summer and she and Rachel have watched the show three more times this week alone. She recognizes every song lyric in real-life conversation, just like I do.

"No. They actually want me to stay a little bit longer. Until January."

"Oh."

"Yeah."

"What do you want to do?"

"I'm not sure," I tell her. But I might be lying.

"Ok."

"Should I stay just so we can actually start saving some money? The new contract will come with a raise."

"You should do what you want to do," she says. I have already been away from home for fifteen months, so she can't really mean I should do what I want to do. She has to have an opinion.

"What do you think I should do?" I ask.

"I think you should do what you want." This conversation is going nowhere unless one of us actually says what is really on our mind.

"I think..." I hesitate to make sure that what I'm saying is actually true. "I think I want to go home. I think I need to go home. To be with you."

A pause.

Then her response. "Oh, thank God!" And she kisses me. It's been a long ride.

384th Show

I am very lucky to have been given the gift of *Jersey Boys*. It has changed me. I am more confident about my ability to create a character that many (including myself) thought was not really right for me. I learned how to physically and mentally work in a long run of a show, and found that I love it. I found relative security in a job for the first time in my life (after I realized I was not going to be fired) and am able to understand how it feels not to worry where the next paycheck will come from. I gained an incredible amount of respect from my peers in New York; they know my drive but never witnessed me have such a gigantic payoff.

And I hope it has changed the way I look for jobs. Prior to *Jersey Boys*, my audition conversations would usually go something like, "Hello! I'm Daniel Robert Sullivan. – No, I'm not working on anything right now. – Well, I finished a run of a new play last month. – No, it doesn't look like the play will ever be produced again..."

Now, my audition conversations will go, "Hello! I'm Daniel Robert Sullivan. – Yes, I was with *Jersey Boys* for a year-and-a-half. – Yes, I will accept your offer of a great role in a Broadway show, thank you!"

At least I hope that is how the conversations will go.

I figure I have about ten months to legitimately claim I have "just finished" my run in *Jersey Boys*. This show is a resume-builder like no other. I am hoping my career will be pushed onward and upward by its status. Well, onward at least. I don't need to go upward.

This experience will stay with me forever. How could it not? Each time the audience stands up (still, every single night) to cheer us on, they are cheering for the underdogs who came out on top. They are cheering for boys from the neighborhood who rocked until their fingers bled and their throats were sore, and were rewarded for it. But they are also cheering for four guys, four Seasons, who struggled with their family lives while they were on the road living their dream. These struggles cannot be discounted.

I've been living my dream on the road this year, too. But I don't want to struggle with my family life anymore. So I'm going to go home. Maybe I'll redo our second bathroom.

Going home is a decision wrought with conflict. While, it is clearly the correct decision for my personal life, I worked for two years just to get this job, so it seems strange to give it up after only a year-and-a-half. Many actors think I'm crazy. I just think my dreams are shifting around a little bit. I give my notice for September 5th, the end of this summer.

I'll tell you, though, I am going to go home with a damn good pile of memories. Four seasons worth of memories, actually.

425th Show

Our dressing rooms each have a monitor through which we can listen to both the show and any announcements made by our stage managers. It is traditional for a stage manager to make a brief announcement immediately following each performance, an announcement that thanks us, perhaps comments on the night's audience ("They seemed hesitant at first, but boy we got 'em at the end!"), and reminds us of the call time for our next show. Most often, this announcement happens while I am in the shower removing the gallons of gel from my hair. Tonight, I decide to watch the band's final playoff from the wings after my curtain call, so I arrive to my dressing room later than usual.

I am removing my tie when the announcement begins. "Hey guys, listen up. The producers are here and they have called a meeting. Please change and meet in the theatre. Full cast and crew, please."

It is almost 11:00 at night and a meeting at this time is very strange. In fact, a last-minute meeting in the theatre is strange anytime because it puts the crew, the ushers, and stage management behind in their schedules.

I've heard about this kind of meeting. This kind of late-night meeting only happens if producers want to get the word out about something before an early-morning press release. And there is only one piece of news that would warrant an early-morning press release two years into a show's run.

I undress, shower, and change very quickly now. A sense of foreboding has begun. I don't know for sure what is about to be announced, but I have a good guess.

Walking into the theatre, I am instinctually drawn to Jeff Madden and Michael Lomenda, two Seasons who actually live in Toronto. I am a guest here in this city. They make their living here; it is their home. They are sure to be hit hardest by whatever comes of this announcement. And the forlorn look on each producer's face tells me my guess is correct.

The theatre is quiet. Introspective. (I'm not the only one to have figured out what this meeting is about.) The producers stand at the foot of the stage. The entire company gathers close together: actors, musicians, stagehands, dressers, hair stylists. I don't think I have ever actually seen all of these people in the same room before.

"Hello, everyone." Aubrey Dan, president and founder of the Dancap Productions producing team, begins speaking. "For the past two months, we have been promoting *Jersey Boys* with vigor unlike anything Toronto has seen before. This summer is well-sold, but we were hoping for a big push into the fall and winter season. This push never materialized. Now that we have sold more than a million tickets, and now that *Jersey Boys* has become the longest running show in the history of this theatre, I am sorry to say that our two-year anniversary performance will also be our last. *Jersey Boys: Toronto* will close on August 22nd."

Silence.

A few tears. Not overly dramatic tears, but the kind of tears you shed when you must say goodbye to something you love.

Some more silence.

This theatre, this show, became a second home to most of us. The fulfillment of a dream that most of us have had since we were young. And, unlike me, most of these people are living their dream right here in their home city. That's the thing that makes it completely fulfilling for them. I've had a dream job in the wrong city; they've had it in the right one.

There's not much talk. Everyone leaves to deal with the news in their own way. There is budgeting to be considered, auditions to be prepared, and maybe even day jobs to look for. I put a hand on the shoulders of both Jeff and Michael. I feel they are losing the most.

Coming back to the apartment, I share the news with Cara. She is dumbstruck, for the show has been selling very well and seems 100% successful. But Toronto is different from New York. In New York, there are many mega-musicals that play for years and years. In Toronto, there has been only three: *The Phantom of the Opera*, *Mamma Mia*, and *Joseph and the Amazing Technicolor Dreamcoat*. Behind these obvious successes lies an elite group of two- or three-year runs: *Cats*, *Miss Saigon*, *The Lion King*, etc. *Jersey Boys* is in this elite group. It is an enormous success in a city that doesn't often support long-running hits; a city that has eight or nine new musicals come through every year, but only a handful that have ever found an audience for more than a couple months.

I tingle with the excitement of being able to play the closing performance, and quickly feel guilty for feeling this excitement. While it will be an honor to end my own journey with the show in such a powerful way, it is not the way I would choose.

430th Show

At the theatre, the entire cast seems drawn to the irony of me giving my notice and then discovering that the show will close two weeks before I was to leave. I joke that the show just could not go on without me. One friend tells me that his first thought on hearing the closing announcement was that he is glad I will be the one closing the show with the company. It is a plot twist in the final act that surprises us all.

And I thought it would be the last such twist.

In my career as an actor, I miss countless weddings, funerals, graduations, and birthdays. Every time an important event is announced, I quickly try to figure out if there is any way I can participate, but usually the answer is that I cannot. I am entitled to some days off, but with very limiting conditions. Today, my wife and I wake up at dawn to watch a live, streaming broadcast of the Emmy Award nominations. Today, having moved up the ranks in the *Saturday Night Live* hair department enough to be included, Cara is nominated for an award. A real Emmy Award. The red carpet, a limousine, the Nokia Theatre, a formal ball, and, quite possibly, a statuette with her name on it, will all be part of her life on August 21st, the day before *Jersey Boys* closes in Toronto. A day on which no one from the show is permitted to take off.

431st Show

I need to find a way to be at the Emmys. Our producers already made it clear that no one will be granted any time off in the days before closing. There will be a lot of press, a lot of very full houses, and a lot of actors with similar unused personal days desiring time off before their struggle for the next gig begins. I have two options: I can beg to be granted an exception to their rule, or I can be dishonest and call in "sick" while at the Emmy Awards (hoping that I am not seen on television).

The *Jersey Boys* producers all along have treated me extremely well and very fairly, so I am not at all comfortable with the dishonest option. On the other hand, I have been very loyal and supportive to my wife all along too, and I am not at all comfortable with not being in Los Angeles to see her (possibly) win her first major award.

Cara and I talk it out. I present her with the argument I could make to the producers, and she believes it is strong enough to warrant an exception to the rules. Hesitantly, I agree. I take the gamble, and present a request for two days off so that I can get to California for the awards and back to Toronto in time for our last day of shows. I include a note that reads as follows:

> *Please know that I realize I am asking for a very big favor. This morning, my wife was nominated for an Emmy Award for her work on* Saturday Night Live. *It is her first nomination, and the ceremony is the afternoon of August 21st. I will just die if I'm not there!*

In retrospect, saying "I will just die if I am not there" puts my vernacular back at grade-school level. I think I was trying to be cute. (I'm pretty sure I failed.) The note continues:

> *Since I began rehearsals in April of 2009, I have not had a single sick day. I think I am the only cast member to go fifteen months without missing a show due to illness. With all my flights to and from New York, I have never missed a show or even been late for a call. I have flown back to Toronto very early every Tuesday to make sure I would be safely at the theatre in time. I had a cyst removed from my tonsil in May, but chose to do it during my vacation week so I would not have to call in sick. My vacation was spent recovering.*
> *If you let me, I will fly back to Toronto on August 21st after the award ceremony, leaving me plenty of time to be here for both of our final shows on August 22nd.*

171

Thank you!

Did you catch the part about the cyst on my tonsil? Did you catch the fact that this cyst was not mentioned when I wrote about my vacation days earlier? I was, and remain, embarrassed by this unusual thing that developed on my left tonsil and began affecting my singing and eating. I knew I had to get it taken care of, but I didn't want to miss any shows or draw attention to my already insecure singing voice. So I scheduled laser surgery for the first day of my vacation, then flew to New York to recover. I couldn't eat solid food. Cara and I went out to a Mexican restaurant and I sucked soft guacamole off the chips. It was a bit gross. I went to the *Saturday Night Live* wrap party and couldn't say anything to Lorne Michaels, not because I didn't have anything to say, but because it hurt to talk. But by the time I was back in Toronto, I was feeling better than ever.

And now I hope this personal revelation will work in my favor with the producers.

440th Show

A text message from my production stage manager arrives: *Dan, your days off have been approved for August 20th and 21st.* Honesty worked! I'm going to the Emmys with Cara. The Canadian producers and Richard Hester, the production supervisor who coached me well for my final audition oh so long ago, have given me one incredibly generous last gift. I will travel to California on the 20th, attend the Emmys, then travel through the night to arrive in time for our final two performances of *Jersey Boys* on the 22nd. What a weekend that will be.

443rd Show

As the end of our show draws closer, the newspapers and blogs alight with the news. The *Toronto Star* calls us an "incredible success" and remarks that the show has made Toronto-Based actor Jeff Madden a star. *Jersey Boys* fans from around the world begin making plans to attend our final show. Many of these fans attended the closing performance of the Chicago Company of *Jersey Boys* and recall that there were four standing ovations during the show. A final press release goes out, and full-color photographs of the four of us Seasons begin appearing in all the publications around the city. Friends and family that have not seen the show yet begin clamoring for reservations. And all I can do is talk about how excited I am about Cara's Emmy nomination.

477th Show

After completing a week of packing and shipping things back to New York (including a huge box of *Jersey Boys* memorabilia), Cara and I fly to Los Angeles for the 62nd Primetime Emmy® Awards. We leave Toronto at 4:30 a.m., squeeze in as much sleep as we can on the plane, grab a taxi, and begin our quick trip through sandy palm trees on our way to the Ritz Carlton at Marina Del Ray. The trip is paid for by NBC, and I am feeling really, really proud of this girl by my side. The sun is shining, a steady breeze is blowing, and we are ready to take on the world.

Then our cab slams into a Toyota Camry and we have to stand on the dusty side of the road with two giant pieces of luggage and a *Jersey Boys* hat.

After making it to the hotel alive and humbled (in a new cab), we walk the beach and have dinner. We set the morning's alarm for an hour that leaves us both time to load our hair with thirty-three of the most perfect hair products on the planet, all of which have traveled with us today. (Being an Emmy-nominated hairdresser means Cara will need to focus on her hair as art, and I shall do the same. This takes time. And bottles upon bottles of hair product.)

The morning of the awards begins with very pricey room-service coffee and two bowls of oatmeal. (Oatmeal is the cheapest thing on the menu.) By the time we're done, Cara looks stunning in green silk and a controlled explosion of perfectly highlighted blond hair, and I look pretty regular in a suit that I got for free at a *Jersey Boys* promotional event. My hair is slicked back just like I wear it in the show, but with much more expensive products this time.

Ready to ride to the Emmy Awards in style!

©*Daniel Robert Sullivan*

We jump in the NBC limousine that is waiting to take us downtown for the ceremony. The limo is stocked full of drinks, but I suggest we hold back for fear of spillage. Cara squeezes my hand in thanks for this suggestion when, not five minutes later, a drink spills all over one of the women at the other end of the car.

The ride takes about twenty minutes, and Cara is nervous. It's kind of fun to see her nervous for something. Usually it is me with trembling hands, now it is her turn. I tell her how unbelievable it feels to be here with her. And so early in her career! If we are at the Emmy Awards now, who knows where we could be in ten years? It doesn't matter if she wins. It is an absolute honor and privilege to be here.

Oh, who am I kidding? I'm going to be really pissed if she doesn't win.

The limo approaches the Nokia Theatre and I can see the red carpet. Our driver inches closer. A pause. He inches even closer. Another pause. There are a lot of limos and they all inch along. The line of limos must be a hundred yards long. We inch some more.

Finally, we pull around a corner and can see the beginning of the red carpet on the other side of the road. But the limo stops. An attendant approaches and opens our door, but we're not sure if we should get out here. After all, the road is busy and the red carpet is on the other side of it.

"Ok, come on out!" The attendant shouts inside to us.

"But..."

"That's it, come on! Right over there!" And she points to the red carpet on the other side of the busy road.

Have you ever played Frogger?

Can you imagine playing Frogger in real life, in formal outfits and on your way to the red carpet?

We dodge luxury cars and limousines as we cross the street, darting left, right, and forward to make it through each lane safely. Cara is a bit slower than I, excusable only because of her heels. Reaching the other side, we encounter...what's this? A line? No, more of a mob. A mob of people trying to get down the red carpet and into the awards ceremony; all of them crammed together in dark suits and long dresses in the hundred degree Los Angeles sun.

This is not quite as glamorous as I imagined.

Sweating profusely, we are finally pushed and shoved to the front. The reason for the mob scene is that only a handful of people are allowed on the red carpet at a time, an effort to make the event seem calm and unrushed. But the reality is that, just off to the left, Neil Patrick Harris' brow is dripping while he waits for his turn.

When our turn arrives, we try to seem dignified. Cara succeeds. I decide that dignity is not worth the effort and begin obnoxiously snapping photos of the paparazzi, of Cara, and of the miniscule Kristin Chenoweth walking in front of me. I also find it fun to try to stick my head in as many real celebrity photos as I can. (I succeed, and there are many photos for sale on Getty Images that have me in the background.)

175

The inside of the Nokia Theatre is gargantuan. It could fit the entire *Jersey Boys* set in its Row F. When we walk in, there is a director onstage asking the audience to laugh and clap with varying degrees of enthusiasm. This is a camera trick. Producers will splice in this footage later when they want a reaction on the broadcast to appear bigger than it actually was. The *Saturday Night Live* nominees are all seated next to each other, and we sit down as the production begins.

Best Editing for a Live Show or Special. Best Directing for a Single Camera Series. Best Sound Engineering for a Show with Betty White in it. The awards keep coming, but I can hardly pay attention once the category is named. I'm waiting. Both of our hands are sweaty.

A camera crew walks the aisles and films people as their names are called to receive an award. It's funny, the crew always seems to be standing in the correct place to capture the first moments of a winner's reaction. Hmm.

Finally, we hear it. "The nominees for Best Hairstyling for A Multi-Camera Series or Special are..." We know who the nominees are. We've been studying them for weeks. We know that the big competition is *Dancing with the Stars*, and I am checking them all out on the far side of the auditorium.

A moment of suspense as the list of nominees comes to a close.

The camera crew comes alert.

The camera crew moves to the far aisle.

The far aisle is where *Dancing with the Stars* is sitting.

"And the Emmy Award goes to...*Dancing with the Stars*!" I squeeze Cara's hand. Maybe it was coming too easy, right? Maybe. But it still would have been cool to stare at that Emmy on my kitchen counter while eating waffles in the morning.

Immediately following the ceremony, we walk through a very unglamorous hallway and cross a very unglamorous back road to attend the official Governor's Ball. Cara's hopes were high, but she takes the disappointment well. We have a nice glass of wine while listening to an incredible big band. We have dinner and move to the dance floor where the guys from *Mythbusters* seem to be having a good time. Then, an announcement:

"Ladies and gentlemen, please put your hands together for tonight's featured entertainment: The Valli Boys!" Four guys in red jackets take the stage and launch into a medley of "Sherry," "Big Girls Don't Cry," and "Walk Like A Man." They are a Four Seasons tribute group. I'm not even joking.

After a few hours at the ball, it is time for me to grab a cab (I choose the one that seems the least accident-prone) and get to the airport for my red-eye flight back to Toronto. I looked nice in this suit earlier today, but now I am disheveled, sweating, and perhaps a bit bloated. (Belts always make me bloated. Women are so lucky they don't have to wear belts. Spanx, maybe. But not belts.) After a full night at the 62nd Primetime Emmy® Awards, and on my way to finish my starring role in the biggest musical hit of the decade, I squeeze into the middle seat of Delta's Row 34 next to a man already snoring and a woman chomping through a foot long salami sandwich.

478th Show

I arrive back in Toronto with only an hour to spare before our first show of the day. The last day. I have not slept well, of course, but I expect some excitement to kick in and rev me up.

The excitement never kicks in. While I convince myself that tonight's show will provide that excitement because of the many die-hard fans in attendance, this matinee actually feels quite somber. This performance is the long goodbye. Tonight may be raucous, so this afternoon we live in each moment a breath longer to be certain we remember it. In just a few hours, we close a story that has inspired us all. In just a few hours, we dismantle a company of artists that will perform this story for the last time together.

479th Show

At 5:30 p.m., "Hey guys, we don't mean to interrupt, but we just wanted to say good luck to you. We drove up from New Jersey to see you tonight!"

It is dinnertime and the four of us Seasons are having a last meal together.

At 5:32 p.m., "Pardon me, gentlemen. Would you mind signing this for us?"

It is dinnertime and the four of us Seasons are trying to process the end of a dream fulfilled.

At 5:35 p.m., "Dan, Michael, Jeff, and Quinn all at one table! OMG, will you please come and say hi to our group at the back?!"

It is dinnertime and the four of us Seasons are having the last conversation we will ever have alone together. Ever.

At 5:39 p.m., "Hi, guys. I don't know if you remember me, but I met you at the stage door last year. I don't mean to interrupt, but I just wanted to thank you for a great run. I've seen you almost thirty times now."

At 5:41 p.m., "Excuse me, are you the Four Seasons?"

At 5:44 p.m., "Holy crap! You're all here! Hey, we have a group of eight over there. Can we get you all to sign these tickets? Do you have a pen?"

At 5:47 p.m., "Hello, gentlemen. We came up from California to see you again tonight. Good luck to you."

At 5:50 p.m., "Boys! We got these balloons for you! Have fun tonight! Can we get a picture?"

At 5:51 p.m., "Hello. I know we haven't met, but I just needed to tell you that we've seen your show forty times now and wanted to give you these stuffed animals. You guys are amazing."

At 5:53 p.m., "Here, I made this collage for each of you. I hope you don't mind carrying it back to the theatre. Mind posing for a picture?"

At 5:56 p.m., "Excuse me, may I get in a picture with you?"

At 5:57 p.m., "Oh, I just had to say something. You all are the best. May I get in a picture with you?"

At 5:58 p.m., "Hey, as long as you're doing pictures, can I get in one, too?"

It is dinnertime, and the four of us Seasons should have just gotten food delivered!

This is an experience like I have never had. I am able to eat only half of my meal before so much time has gone by that I must return to the theatre. The four of us have not been able to have a private conversation. We have not had a single moment alone together to process what this experience has meant for us. We have not even had time to order a second iced tea. What we have had is the smallest (ever so tiny) taste of what Brad and Angelina must go through every time they go out. And I hereby vow never to chase Angelina for a picture again.

On my walk back to the theatre, while on the phone with my mother, I am stopped three times and asked for pictures and given gifts. Three times. While on the phone. This is getting ridiculous. Don't these people know that I am just a small-time actor from New York, one of thousands? Don't they know that next week I will probably be ordering off the dollar menu at McDonald's and wondering if I'll ever work again? And don't they know that I am on the phone?

I sign in at the theatre for the last time and try to analyze my thoughts a bit. I am grateful for the attention. It is flattering. But it is also unbelievably overwhelming. I would love to spend a few minutes meeting each fan and thanking them for being so kind, but that takes at least three minutes to do. I have encountered about fifty such fans in the past hour, and an hour is all the dinner break I have. Simple math will tell you that I should just be hiding in my dressing room.

I go through my usual routine preparing for the show and finish earlier than usual. The other three guys finish early too, perhaps sensing that we didn't really have the moment we wanted to have back at dinner. We gather now in Michael's dressing room for a hug. A couple gifts. A few words. Hmm. This is not as dramatic as I imagined.

A life in the theatre is a life of goodbyes. I came to that realization a long time ago. And you know something? Those goodbyes harden you. I care about these guys and I know that this show has changed each of our lives in dramatic ways, but the goodbye is easier than I expected. For all of us.

Is that what professionalism brings about? A hardening of the heart when a job comes to a close?

We take our places for the beginning of the show.

The standard pre-show announcement brings silence to the crowd. I give thumbs-up to the guys I can see from my vantage upstage in the dark. The first chords of music begin and there is a roar. A loud roar. But I expected that; the fans are out in full-force. The intro song plays stronger than ever, then it fades out as I snap and slide downstage for my first speech. And then my world stops.

The cheers are so loud that I cannot hear the band. I can see our sound engineer fiddling with his computers to make the band even louder, but his system is maxed out already. The cheers are so loud that I cannot hear the guys next to me who are singing "ah, ah, doo-doo" practically in my ear. What can I do but wait? I stand there, staring down the stream of spotlight now blinding my eyes, and I wait. Ten seconds. Twenty seconds. Thirty, forty, fifty. The cheers continue, louder than before. Finally, I hold up a finger. Just one finger. And they stop.

We continue the show with equal energy on both sides of the footlights. The performance is not technically any different than any other we've done all year, but it does have a certain boost of power behind it. If there were another ten medleys in the first act, I'm sure I would have the energy to do them tonight. If there were even higher notes written in Frankie Valli's songs, I'm sure Jeff Madden would be able to hit them tonight. We receive a standing ovation after "Sherry." Another after "Walk Like A Man." Another at the intermission. Another after "Can't Take My Eyes Off Of You." And a raucous one after "Who Loves You." I have been a part of countless standing ovations in my life, but they've always come at the end of a performance; never have I experienced them during a show. Some members of the audience are Tweeting during the performance:

- "Standing ovations throughout the show, applause at random intervals, autographs, tears, and thong-throwing. Bye-bye *Jersey Boys*, it's been fun!" (@shelbygilmore)

- "Intermission now...the crowd is insane and I'm a part of it! Ha-ha." (@celineolivia)

- "THAT WAS THE BEST TOILET SCENE YET! I love me some *Jersey Boys*!" (@jensmiith)

- "The audience just lost their shit!" (@elenajuatco)

At the final curtain call, I wave goodbye to the crowd, give a nod to the band, and wrap arms with the three other Seasons as we run offstage. But we don't leave the wings just yet. It is still loud out there; the audience is still on their feet. We stick around to listen to the band's final playoff and the energy is palpable. We played our final show with an extra kick of stamina, but the band plays it with an extra kick of skill.

They were a cohesive group already, but never have they sounded so together and so full of heart. The audience feels this, I think, because they are dancing with abandon out there in the dark.

When the band finishes, they exit the stage and we all congratulate each other. The house lights come up, the stage lights go down, and the backstage lights rise a bit to let us all see each other on our way out. A few minutes of goodbyes. A walk to the back hallway. Another few minutes of shared amazement. A walk to my dressing room. Another few minutes removing my microphone and washing my face. Then a knock on the door.

Full Company

"Dan, they are still out there." A stagehand has made his way to our wing of dressing rooms. He calls for the other three Seasons. "Seriously, they aren't stopping."

What is he referring to?

The four of us follow this stagehand back to the wings and can now see that, ten minutes after the band has left the stage, fifteen minutes after we have taken our final bow, the audience is still on their feet and not one of them has budged. The ushers have opened the doors, the chain-link fence curtain has been lowered, the lights onstage have been completely shut off...and still the audience remains.

We are not sure what to do. A concert performer receiving such an ovation would surely come back onstage for an encore. But we are not concert performers. And we don't even have microphones anymore, never mind an encore prepared. And because *Jersey Boys* staging is so particular, so specific, we are not even sure if we would be allowed to step onstage again. And yet the audience does not leave.

After too much time decision-making, it is the stagehand (thank you, Brent) who finally tells us we had better just get out there...now. So we do. With arms around each other again, Jeff, Michael, Quinn, and I walk out to the middle of the stage to an eruption that tops everything we've already felt. There are handmade signs out there. There are flowers being thrown onto the stage. There are people crying in the front row. And wait, there are people crying onstage, too. Four of us, I think.

Final curtain call on closing night. Jeff Madden, me, Michael Lomenda, Quinn VanAntwerp.

©*Aubrey Dan*

We can do nothing but stand there and take it in. No one would hear us if we were to speak, and what would we say anyway? This reaction is not, could never possibly be, for us. This reaction is for the story that resonates so deeply for everyone in the room. Each seat out there is filled with someone who has some kind of dream, and some kind of obstacle standing in its way. The story of the Four Seasons proves that those obstacles can be overcome if you set your sights dead-ahead. I don't mean to sound preachy or New Age or something, but I really do believe that is what connects people to *Jersey Boys*. Jeff, Michael, Quinn, and I are good performers, but let us call a spade a spade: we are not the ones inspiring such a reaction! I want to cheer right along with the audience tonight. I want to yell and scream and jump up and down and shout, "I know! I know why you love this thing so much! I know why you come back time and time again! I know it is because we all need to be reminded constantly that we can do what we have dreamed about! We need to be reminded constantly never ever to give up!"

I want to jump up and down and say this stuff, but I don't. I just get a little teary. I get teary because in front of me is absolute proof that, after all these years of trying, I finally got to where I wanted so much to be. With a smile, I think, "What the hell am I going to do now?"

EPILOGUE

I have appeared as Tommy DeVito four hundred and seventy-nine times. Now, as I board the plane that will take me back to New York, I think I like him even more than I have for the past few years.

Tommy DeVito is a confident gambler. And I'm taking a gamble, too. I am gambling that this will not be the last show I ever perform in, but only the most recent. I am gambling that I do not need to jump right back into a full schedule of teaching right away, that maybe another big acting job will come along (or this book will sell). I am gambling that the producers of this show will not discredit me for having wanted to leave the job without any more incentive than "personal reasons." But Tommy DeVito is also a guy who dreams big. He often gets what he wants simply because he doesn't give up. He knows that you have to work hard, struggle, and often sacrifice things on your journey towards a dream. I feel like I did just that with my dream of getting into *Jersey Boys*. I worked hard. I struggled. I sacrificed. And it paid off, didn't it?

Cara is sitting beside me as our plane lifts off the ground. I wish I could say that her Emmy Award was sitting on my lap, but maybe next year. Toronto creeps out beneath me one last time and the CN Tower holds my gaze just like it did the day I arrived. This city has been good to me. It has made me a (very small and hardly worth mentioning) star. It has given me a pile of new friends, good and kind people who have intimidated me with their talents four hundred and seventy-nine times. It has fulfilled my childhood dream. Now it's time to attend to something else.

There has been another dream running around my head since I left home seventeen months ago. A simpler one. A dream that requires only my presence, not two years of auditions (or two hundred pages). This other dream is simply to be able to spend my nights falling asleep at home in the arms of my wife. To be working in the same city again is what we both need. That'll be enough for a while. Other dreams will come along, surely, but this one needs attention now.

"Daniel, I think I'm going to take a nap during this flight."

"Cara, I think I will too, because that's my next little dream."

"What is?"

"To fall asleep next to you most of my nights."

"Aw. That's nice. Cheesy, but nice."

A pause.

"Cara?"

"Yes?"

"Thanks for being so supportive of all of this. You are totally my best friend." She moves in closer.

"Daniel?"

"Yeah, hon?"

"You're my best friend, too."

Another pause.

"G'night."

"G'night."

And home we go.

AFTERWORD

In the years following the closing of *Jersey Boys* in Toronto, I have remained a part of the Jersey family. Shortly after my return to New York, I was asked if I could travel to the Bahamas to perform selections from the show at a publicity event. A month later, I did the same thing in Berlin. Next was Morocco, but by this time my family caught on to the fact that they could benefit from the free hotel room, so Cara and Rachel joined me in our first trip to Africa. The international recognition of the show was letting my little family see the world. Shortly afterwards, the three of us went to Paris together because of *Jersey Boys*. Rachel had been taking French classes at school, and she cried when she saw the Eiffel Tower for the first time. To say I'm grateful for what this show has given me would be a tremendous understatement.

But the journey didn't get easier.

"Dan, would you be interested in playing Tommy for a while in New Zealand?"

"Thanks for agreeing to that New Zealand thing, Dan, but we don't need you after all. That said, we are launching the 2nd National Tour soon. Would you like to audition again?"

"We all love you, Dan, but you're just not a great fit for this tour. Now this one's a long shot because we have another guy in mind, but would you like to come audition for Tommy on Broadway?"

"Sorry, Dan. Some of the team just doesn't think you look like a Tommy."

I'd heard that before. So I went back to acting in smaller shows. I taught many classes. I wrote a play, *Prospect High: Brooklyn*. I continued to sing for the show's publicity events, but playing Tommy in *Jersey Boys* seemed to be an unattainable goal all over again. Then, after four years:

"Hey Dan, we'd like to offer you the role of Tommy in Las Vegas."

And every dream is reignited.

APPENDICES

APPENDIX I

SUPERFANS

A fan of the show made us these personalized bears!

©Daniel Robert Sullivan

On April 10th, 2010, a college student in Ontario named Frances Fong-Lee saw her hundredth performance of Jersey Boys. *As a gift, the producers bought out the entire front row for Frances, and she filled it with other superfans who were closing in on her record. What is it about* Jersey Boys *that keeps these fans coming back? What does the show mean to them, personally? I tracked down some of the superfans and asked them to answer in their own words:*

"I've been a lifelong Four Seasons fan, but never knew their story. I love how the show ends with each Season having an opportunity to talk about their life now. It's especially satisfying after seeing their struggles. Now, so many years later, these guys and their families are again in the spotlight and reaping the rewards for their life's work. It's a true story and a very captivating one. Frankie is still performing and I've seen him several times since being introduced to *Jersey Boys*. Seeing him perform reinforces the belief that despite whatever obstacles or setbacks you encounter, you can get through it. It is inspirational.

"I've met several other fans of the show, and we've had fan gatherings at various *Jersey Boys* events. I've formed friendships with people of all ages, from teens to seniors, and we all have a common interest: a love for this show."

–Linda SooHoo (San Francisco, CA)

"Dan, I had no knowledge of pop music prior to October, 1962. During that month, at eleven years old, I was hospitalized for a week and my roommate was a teenage fellow who played WABC radio constantly, and I heard 'Sherry' over and over. As a gift while I was recovering, my father bought me 'Sherry and 11 Others', my first LP. I followed the Four Seasons throughout the 1960s. By the early 70s, the Four Seasons' music faded from the charts. But on November 30, 1974, my father and I were in our car and heard 'My Eyes Adored You' for the first time, and we talked about how we hadn't heard from Frankie or the Seasons for a long time and this was a beautiful re-entry. My father died in an accident two days later, and the song still reminds me of him each time I hear it.

"During 2005–2006, I spent most of my time in Europe on business. I had just returned from Munich literally a few minutes before Christian Hoff won his Tony over heavily favored Jim Dale for his role of Tommy. His beautiful speech in memory of his dad made me think of that last day with my dad. I bought a ticket on eBay the next day to that Wednesday's matinee.

"Like everyone else was, I was floored by the performances and the play. I was glad the theatre was dark, since I actually cried during 'My Eyes Adored You' and 'Fallen Angel.' I was especially awed by Christian's performance after hearing his powerful speech, and I emailed him that evening via his website, telling him about my dad. Lo and behold, he answered me within a few minutes, saying 'I never imagined my Tony win would touch someone so deeply.'

"I couldn't believe that an actor winning the biggest award on Broadway would take precious time to acknowledge someone he'd never met. Of course, his response gave me the impetus to see the show again. I'd been to stage doors where some stars rush out to the waiting limos, with little time to greet the fans. These guys were the exact opposite...they didn't leave until every fan was acknowledged, every playbill signed, and every picture taken. They knew me by name almost immediately.

"Although I've lost count, I estimate I've seen the show about forty times. Having been a CPA and traveling the country for the better part of thirty-five years, a lot of friends visit me in New York and I visit many others. Although seeing other shows is enticing, I absolutely know that my friends will love *Jersey Boys* and, as icing on the cake, will be treated like royalty at the stage door.

"Going back to the first time I met Christian Hoff after our exchanging a few emails, when I extended my hand, Christian took it and proceeded to hug me with his free arm and ask me about my life and career. In those few minutes, he showed me that he not only liked me, but that he cared. Initially, I thought the caring was unique to Christian, but I see now that it is a wonderful trait of many of the cast members and creative team, who are so grateful to be involved with such a wonderful production and so appreciative of their fans.

"You know, at this stage of life these last four years seem like a fairy tale that I still don't believe, but am just enjoying. Not only will the cast and crew look back upon this as a wonderful time in their lives, but I will too, Dan."

–Howard Tucker (Staten Island, NY)

"The cast is amazing. There's something about them that makes them loveable; even if they were to mess up onstage, you wouldn't care. Plus, I have a huge admiration for swings and understudies, so I want to try and catch all of them in their different roles! I think I've seen almost every understudy, and it still blows my mind how one person can be so flawless in all three or four of his/her roles.

"Originally, the underdog story is what got me. The fact that four guys who no one thought had a chance made it big was really inspiring to me; it gives me hope for myself. In my run of forty shows, though, I find I've met a lot of other fans who I don't know what I'd do without. Even certain cast members have come to mean a lot to me.

"After a while, it stops being about the show and more about what you recognize in the little intricacies onstage that you never noticed before. I'm still noticing new things. The writers of this show are pure genius.

"This show helped to broaden my horizons, both in the world of theatre and my own understanding of life itself. It has made me fall in love with the stage, and even compelled me to practice singing, dancing, and running lines of other plays or movies so one day I may be ready to perform myself. I've memorized every step, every word, every costume change, every set change; they may as well throw me in as a swing! Everyone has to see *Jersey Boys*. It has changed my life, and I guarantee it will change yours in some form or another."

–Michelle Bozzetto (Brampton, ON)

"It is hard to explain exactly why anyone sees the same show over and over again. I feel like *Jersey Boys* is a collection of so many fantastic things—the music and songs, the true story that the show is based on, and the talented actors—all of which are the things that keep me going back to the show an endless number of times. The music and songs are absolutely electric! It makes me feel like I am involved in a musical experience, rather than just simply watching a Broadway show. I love how timeless the songs are, and that they are still relevant and popular today.

"What brings this already incredible show to another level is the absolutely gifted cast. The cast is what brings the story and songs to life night after night. The personality, charisma, and talent that the four lead guys bring to their respective roles are completely unmatched; there is nothing quite like it. It is all of this greatness within one show that makes me want to see *Jersey Boys* again and again.

"*Jersey Boys* truly means happiness to me. There is a certain kind of happiness that goes along with seeing this show. Leaving the theatre with a huge smile and being filled with joy is one of the best experiences anyone going to a theatre performance can ask for. When leaving the show, I am always grinning from ear-to-ear and my face hurts from smiling so much. "'Happiness' is the best way to describe what the show has brought to my life. It is a special feeling that I always get while attending *Jersey Boys*. And the casts rock! They are some of the most talented people in the business, and are some of the nicest and most genuine people I have had the pleasure to meet. They are not only vibrant onstage, but off stage as well."

–Amanda Timm (Newmarket, ON)

"I have always enjoyed the storyline because it rings true. I'm not really one for fiction, so this story speaks to me. I was born in 1961 and I remember my dad playing this music around the house. Because this is a 'period piece,' it brings back so many memories of my parents when they were young adults. For example, my mom had similar dresses and hairstyles, and everybody went bowling all the time! I remember watching the *Ed Sullivan Show* in black and white, and my parents often went to the Roostertail, as we lived in Detroit at the time. So for me, *Jersey Boys* is a little slice of my childhood that I can relive again and again.

"It introduced me to the Broadway community in a way I wouldn't have otherwise benefited from. I enjoy meeting the actors (as well as the crew and other people associated with the show) at the stage door. I enjoy learning about professional theatre and I especially enjoy attending cabarets, open-mics and showcases by past and present cast members. It's great to see them display their many talents outside of the show.

"We try and follow our favorites as best we can in an appreciative and non-intrusive way. In fact, some actors have become friends. In addition, I have made many great friends who are also fans. We have dinners, parties, fan get-togethers, and even the occasional bickering, so in that way we truly are an extended family!

"It's never the same show twice for me and I have the same enthusiasm on the 43rd show as I did on the very first one. Once I hear the opening notes of 'Oh, What A Night,' the charge comes right back. I have seen twenty different actors play Frankie in every company except Australia, and the real thrill for me is seeing new actors in the roles we have come to know and love. Several other *Jersey Boys* fans and I often quote lines from the show when the timing is right and it always garners a hearty laugh! Most of them, of course, come from Tommy or Crewe. Elice and Brickman sure gave you guys some great material with which to work!"

–Gary Neuberg (New York, NY)

"Being a big Frankie Valli & the Four Seasons fan, the music always takes me to a better place! *Jersey Boys* has the combination of the greatest music, along with a story that makes you laugh, cry, and root for four guys with all odds against them. From the minute I saw it back at La Jolla Playhouse in 2004, I predicted to my husband that *Jersey Boys* would win Best Musical at the Tony Awards and so would Christian Hoff for Best Supporting Actor. It was an amazing experience to watch such a masterpiece in La Jolla. So great, in fact, that my husband (who also loved the show, but is not quite as nuts as I am) suggested that we create *Jersey Boys Blog* (jerseyboysblog.com).

"The following year, it was electrifying to see *Jersey Boys* on Broadway, and each and every time that I've seen it on Broadway and all over the country it's been like a completely new experience; I am always discovering something new about the music, the lines, the nuances onstage, the scenes, and the actors. So, why do I come back again and again? Along with the music and the great story, it's the live theatre experience! Considering it's live theatre, it's always new and I especially love seeing various cast members' portrayals. Each cast member makes the role their own.

"It's meant so much to my life! *Jersey Boys* is a very inspirational story about never giving up on your dreams, no matter how tough it gets. Along with the inspirational story, we have had the phenomenal opportunity to have met and to have interviewed some amazing cast members, crew members, and creative team members. We've also met the real Four Seasons! It's been a dream come true!"

–Susie Skarl (Las Vegas, NV)

"It's an addiction! I can't get enough. Watching *Jersey Boys* makes me smile. When it's done, I want to see it again and again. I love the music, and the great vocals add so much to the experience. I feel like I'm seeing The Four Seasons live in concert.

"The show has practically become a big part of my everyday life. I visit the *Jersey Boys Blog* at least once a day and check out what the *Jersey Boys* cast and fans are up to on Facebook. I've met a lot of *Jersey Boys* fans online and have met a few of them in person. Also, a huge part of my expenses have been related to seeing *Jersey Boys* (wink).

"All of my four trips out of state (Hawaii) last year were to go watch the show. Last year alone, I saw it on Broadway (two trips), Las Vegas, and Chicago (which I visited for the first time and by myself). I'll be going to see it again on Broadway in May and November of this year."

–Nancy J. Dela Cruz (Honolulu, HI)

"This show has meant a lot to me. I really love the story behind the Four Seasons, and who the four members were involved with to get to where they are now. I've made some really good friends thanks to this show, not just friends from Toronto, but in the United States and London as well. The love for this show is so great between our *Jersey Boys* 'family.'

"I would like to thank all the amazing actors and crew members who are involved in any and every production of *Jersey Boys* around the world. It's always so great to see and meet the actors after the show; they are all just so nice to talk to. And it has been such a pleasure to get to know more about the songs and stories behind the Four Seasons."

-Frances Fong-Lee (Richmond Hill, ON)

"My first trip to *Jersey Boys* was for my birthday, four girlfriends running in the rain to make the last bell. We had a most memorable evening. It was elevating! I raved about the show to everyone, and the next week I took my mother and her sister (who was visiting from Ireland). I took my uncle, who couldn't remember the last time he had been out past midnight. I took my great friend Terry who comes once a year to catch some Toronto theatre. Then for Christmas, I went with a friend I met at the stage door. I reconnected on Facebook with a friend from University and we had a fabulous evening in January! I even popped in by myself for a matinee when I came to the city.

"Why do I keep coming back? Guess I found a show that captures all the essential elements of great theatre. For me, it's the music. A tried and tested core of great songs; the story of the inspiration to create them and the drive to perform. It's a depiction of a different time in the music industry. It's also movement. I love the physical drive behind the narration and songs. The simplicity of the set constantly drives the characters and keeps them on the move. Most important: the cast. I'm told there are other cities with other performers doing this show. It's unimaginable! Our cast is magnificent! Every time I have seen this show there has been a memorable moment where one actor sets out the most magical delivery of a line. It would break your bleedin' heart!

"I've taken young people, seniors, friends I haven't seen in years, and people I hardly know. We have all had the most marvelous theatre experience possible, and we are still talking about it. I mean, I know I have brilliant instincts. But it's nice when everyone around you agrees..."

–Nicola Hengst (Little Britain, ON)

APPENDIX II

THE BELMONT TAVERN

As old as the town itself, the Belmont Tavern in Belleville, New Jersey is as authentic an Italian immigrant restaurant experience as you can get. The proprietor, who goes by no more of a name than "Jimmy," knows everything that has ever happened in this part of town, and knew the Four Seasons as they were coming up. My visit to this restaurant, and my experience with Jimmy, was one I will never forget. And now I kind of feel like someday, and that day may never come, Jimmy may call on me to do a service for him...

Belleville, New Jersey. Population: 35,000. Three square miles of congested land stuck between a highway, a landfill, crime-ridden downtown Newark, and a river laced with oil and refuse. From the original French, Belleville means "beautiful city." But one could easily debate the merits of that name.

"Jimmy! My name is Dan and I play Tommy DeVito in the Canadian company of *Jersey Boys*. Your restaurant is famous in our world, and I'd love to come visit. Will you be there on Monday night?" Jimmy is the owner of the Belmont Tavern, a legendary New Jersey institution, and I have heard that he is the guy to talk to if you want to hear stories from back in the day.

"Yeah, I'll be here."

My wife and I arrange to meet our friends Jessica and Kent on Monday night for what I keep calling a "dinner adventure." I remind everyone that I am not sure if this place will be any good; I just feel a need to visit. The restaurant has been around since the early days of the Four Seasons, and is on the short list of places that Tommy DeVito and Frankie Valli still hang out in today.

"Do you think you'll get any special treatment?" Our friends ask this as we jump into their car.

"No. They don't know me or anything. I just want to get a feel for what the place is like. I'm hoping Jimmy will make time to tell us a bit about what the neighborhood was like back in the 50s and 60s, but he might be too busy. Who knows?"

Frankie invited us all to his sound-check before one of his own concerts in Toronto.

©Daniel Robert Sullivan

We drive from Manhattan out into the vast suburbs of New Jersey. We ride in style in an SUV with a sunroof the size of a fresco at the Sistine Chapel. (And our friends humbly insist that the car is not actually an SUV, for an SUV would be a lot bigger. But Cara and I still have room to waltz in the back seat, so I'm not sure I believe them.) We have printed directions from Google, and a GPS for backup. The drive should take twenty minutes at the most.

An hour later we have to call another friend for help.

"Gina, you grew up in New Jersey. How do we get to the Belmont Tavern on Bloomfield Avenue?"

"You guys need to get back on the highway. There are two Bloomfield Avenues, and you're on the wrong one." The suburbs of New Jersey foil Google and GPS with their duplicitous street names.

We get back on the highway, find the correct exit, and quickly pass two boarded-up schools. One of them actually has a sign that reads "Girl's Entrance"

198

over its side door, so I can assume it is a school that has been boarded-up for a long, long time. We ride alongside a river. Or is it a creek? Whatever its label, it is no more than a path of dirty water chunked full of old tires. (Jessica calls it Belleville's Lazy River Ride.)

As we get closer to the center of town, we begin to travel along Tommy DeVito Drive. We pass Tommy DeVito's boyhood home, a typical brick-bottom, wood-top white house at one end of a congested road. And then we see the Belmont.

For all its history and lore, the Belmont Tavern ain't much to look at.

The Belmont is a small, brick building with blinds covering its two front windows, making it impossible to see inside. It is stuck between a West Indian grocery and a live poultry warehouse. There is no one on the dark street as we pull up outside, so we are convinced the place is going to be empty. The Belmont has a few generic beer signs and one placard that touts its famous Chicken Savoy. I have heard that the Chicken Savoy is delicious, but I am feeling a little weird about it now that I see the live poultry warehouse right next door.

We walk slowly to the front door, each of us city-folk a bit wary of what may be on the other side. I step forward to be the first one through, as I am the one that convinced everyone to join me out here in the first place. I open the door, and can instantly sense that the place is jam-packed full of diners. Our adventure begins.

"Daniel Robert Sullivan! Get over here!" Five men drinking at the bar have seen me come in, and they know my name. Now, Jimmy-the-owner is the only person I have spoken to on the phone, and I only gave him my first name. Clearly, these five guys at the bar have Googled me and have memorized my full name.

Their accents are just as strong as I hoped. They are just as boisterous as I imagined. And they are far nicer than I could have asked for.

The guys inundate me with questions, each fighting for a turn to speak. They want to know all about the show up in Canada. They want to know where I am from. They want to tell me about Belleville. They want me to sing. We've been inside only two minutes.

Jimmy fights his way through the guys to introduce himself, and seems genuinely happy that I have arrived. He says it is "real good" to have a Jersey Boy here in the bar, and that he hopes these guys will leave me alone long enough for us to eat. (He doesn't realize that I don't want to be left alone, that I want to visit with all of them.)

Our server comes over to usher us to a table, a prime table in the corner that has been waiting for our arrival. The place really is packed, and we have to maneuver around fifteen checkered tablecloths before reaching our own. The voices in here are loud, accented, and joyous. Every rising tone has the sound of a story that just has to be told.

We order a carafe of chilled Chianti and dive into the menu. I eat Italian food all the time, but I must admit that there are a number of items on this menu that I don't recognize. Actually, the entire third page is made up of items I don't recognize. My group leaves it to me to do the ordering, but I think it smarter to ask for recommendations.

Our server leads us through descriptions of the popular items, and we end up ordering heaps of Shrimp Beeps, Clams Oreganato, and fresh Italian Bread. We follow that with a giant bowl of Ziti Pot Cheese and two overflowing platters of "Mad" Chicken and the famous Chicken Savoy. I choose not to think about the fact that the chicken we are eating was probably an actual resident of "the old neighborhood" just days ago.

As we eat, we are visited by each of the men that greeted me at the bar earlier. They each want their picture taken with me, making me feel like quite the celebrity as I stand up to accommodate each one. They just happen to have a Fuji disposable camera with them, but is it possible that they bought it just for this occasion?

Jimmy's father is the first to come over, and he tells me how he used to watch The Four Lovers play at the Silhouette Club down the street. The Four Lovers was one of the original incarnations of the Four Seasons, and the Silhouette Club features prominently in *Jersey Boys*.

Jimmy comes by to thank me for the autographed show photo I brought for him, and shows us some of the pictures on the wall. Sinatra, DiMaggio, Sammy Davis Jr., Joe Pesci...they've all hung out at the Belmont at one time or another and they've all left kind messages on their framed photographs. Jimmy points out a corner of the bar and says, "By the way, that's the corner where Joe Pesci used to play guitar and sing when he was coming up. He used to play for tips every weekend." Joe Pesci as a solo music act. Who knew?

A cop from Nutley (that's the next town over) comes to introduce himself next. He is an Irish guy, and asks me about how I feel being part of an Italian show when I am obviously Irish, too. This cop grew up down the street from here in the house next door to Nick Massi, one of the original Four Seasons. He says he's always felt like he was in the minority as an Irishman. When he has a picture taken of the two of us Irish boys, he jokes that it should go up on the *Jersey Boys Blog*. (This tells me that these guys actually check out the *Jersey Boys Blog*. That was unexpected.)

Anita from the kitchen comes to check in on us, asking about the Beeps and the Savoy. We tell her the Beeps disappeared too quickly, and we are still debating who gets to eat the last piece of Chicken Savoy.

An older gentleman sits down with us, telling us how he came in tonight because he heard I was going to be here. He just finished playing a game of fast-pitch softball and is tired, but tonight is a special occasion, he says. They love connecting with *Jersey Boys* people. People forget, he tells us, that the Four Seasons struggled ten years in this town before they made it big. They played music every night at one bar or another, trying to make ends meet as best they could. And Frankie Valli, he says, always thanks his hometown when given the opportunity.

The cop comes back, leaning in close to us this time. "You see this guy next to you?" he whispers. "Check out his ankle." His ankle is locked up with a parole bracelet, for this guy is, apparently, a former mob thug who isn't allowed to leave the area. He is eating the biggest bowl of linguini I have ever seen.

We are told that Tommy DeVito was sitting at this very table two weeks ago when he came by for dinner before being inducted into the New Jersey Hall of Fame. While here, Tommy was reminiscing about robbing the department store across the street three times while he was growing up. This department store used to be New Jersey's largest supplier of school uniforms for kids, and it is just a block away from where Tommy lived.

Nick Massi's son was also here last week, and spent the entire time talking about his father. This seems typical. The people in this town are proud of the Four Seasons. They are proud of their town. They have a giant American flag behind the bar, but it is clear that the association with their township roots much deeper than any sense of nationalism.

The guys at the bar make us promise to visit again, and we make that promise. Another trip would be mutually beneficial: we get to hear some good stories and they get to view their town as a destination instead of a jumping-off point. While they may be glad the Four Seasons come from here, it seems to really thrill these guys when people come to here.

Plus, if we come here again, we'll get to have more of those Beeps.

APPENDIX III

LINDSAY THOMAS, A FALLEN ANGEL

Although I only had the privilege of meeting her once, no book about Jersey Boys *would be complete without a mention of Lindsay Thomas. Lindsay appeared a few times in my journal entries before I knew her story. But her story has since touched every member of the* Jersey Boys *family.*

Lindsay was born in Edmonton, Alberta and attended the famed musical theatre program at Sheridan College in Toronto, Ontario. Shortly after graduating, Lindsay earned a role in *Hairspray*, performing the show on Broadway, in Toronto, and on the US National Tour. She came back to Canada to perform for several seasons at the Stratford Festival, leaving only when she was cast in *Jersey Boys: Toronto* as Francine.

I am told that her smile around the theatre was infectious, that her laugh filled the entire (very long) hallway. I am told that she treated everyone with respect and admiration, from her directors to the lady who cleaned her dressing room.

But there was something wrong. While she was in great shape and could sing the hell out of anything (especially "My Boyfriend's Back"), Lindsay was feeling sick. Unusually sick. She had a cough that would not go away, and it was not explainable until her doctors discovered Stage IV lung cancer in this 31-year-old girl who, according to her friends, didn't even smoke.

Lindsay whipped off her wig during the few minutes I was able to meet her, glad to show off her funky, bald look. And I'm not going to lie, she looked pretty cute bald. She was feisty, that's for sure. But sadly, she lost her battle with cancer on February 3rd, 2010.

I do not feel right sharing too much about Lindsay, for I am not one who knew her well. But I can attest absolutely and wholeheartedly to the effect she has had on those who work for *Jersey Boys*. She was loved, and she remains loved. She has made many people reconsider their own outlook on life and its uncertainties. She has made many people re-visit the love in their life. And she has made many people appreciate their time in the show, appreciate being able to live their dream while they can. And whenever something seems impossible, all we really need to do is remember Lindsay and all that she could do (all that she could sing) while fighting her faltering health. She sang with love and a smile. Would that we could all manage to do just that.

APPENDIX IV

FULL COMPANY NOTES

This is how many people it takes to put on one performance of Jersey Boys.

This section is for die-hard Jersey Boys *fans only! For a couple of years, Nathan Scherich, a swing with the National Tour and Broadway companies, put together a monthly newsletter for* Jersey Boys *companies worldwide. "The Old Neighborhood" is filled with funny columns for everyone associated with the show to enjoy during their down-time. My contribution to the newsletter was a recurring section of "Full Company Notes," changes in the show that I sarcastically asked cast members to make. If you are a true fan, perhaps you will find some of these notes amusing:*

- All: Trust in this material. You don't need to "act" it. Just lay back and let the words tell the story simply and without too much nuance. Trust that the audience will "get it" and just stay in your dressing rooms all night while we let them read the script silently to themselves.

- All: In the spirit of ensemble-based theatre, the show will now be referred to as *Jersey Boys and Girls. And Thugs. And Knuckles.*

- Knuckles: When you hear "Apple of My Eye," please take a moment to silently rock inside your head. Then, very tenderly, mutter something about "them not writing 'em like that anymore…"

- All: No more new jokes, new beats, or "improvements." The show is frozen. (hee-hee)

- All: In keeping with the show's growth and improvement, certain changes are to be expected. That said, Sunday we will be performing Gypsy.

- Nick Massi: Yes, you may play Mama Rose.

- The Dodgers have convinced America's Got Talent to incorporate a new performance category. "Fake Piano Playing" debuts next week.

- Tommy: If you don't get your exit applause, go back and do your monologue again.

- All: The film version is coming, and will have to have a "name" actor in the principal role. Offers are out to James Gandolfini and Paul Reubens. (Casting Director Merri Sugarman loves Paul Reubens.)

- All: Ok, I made that up about Merri loving Paul Reubens. I mean, she probably did when he was rockin' that psychedelic kid's show, but that porn stuff just put him in the crazy pile.

- Tommy: After your first card trick, show Frankie your upside-down straightjacket escape.

- All: In an attempt to visualize the boys' Catholic background, please genuflect before entering the spiral staircase.

- All: John Lloyd Young has just released a CD of Neil Sedaka covers. Please support.

- Gyp: In an attempt to visualize the boys' Catholic background, please turn the wine into blood at the last supper Sit-Down scene.

- Bob: Line change for consistency…"We make a partnership. I give you half of the first 60% of everything I write, excluding subsidiary compositional changes up to 35% of the initial investment, you give me half of the first two-thirds of everything you record outside the group, except in such instances as original band members gathering in

206

50-50 side projects to produce quick-head arranged Christmas albums." This will make everything clearer.

- Priest in "Fallen Angel": In an attempt to visualize the boys' Catholic background, please X???#X???#X???#X???# X???#. (This note censored by the Archdiocese of Newark, New Jersey.)

- All: Instead of the Seabreeze Lounge, Gyp's club will now be called the Febreze Lounge. But don't tell him.

- All: Production Supervisor Richard Hester says these notes are "global changes." Don'tcha just love it when he says, "global changes?" Aww, Richard, you're so cute. Don't ever change. (Please note that all global changes will change again next month.)

- Norm: After you say, "Tommy's put me in an awkward position," pause as you recall the last awkward position he put you in. The one with the blender.

- All: In light of new historical info, the two women who bring Tommy dinner will now be (1) pregnant and (2) carrying a baby. For the baby, we will use a lifelike doll or (where contractually possible) the actor playing Joe Pesci.

- Tommy: Line change…"Go home. Make your wife happy, even if it takes forty-five minutes to an hour."

- Band: In a money-saving move, all JB companies will have Keyboard Two replaced with that guy who plays the accordion and has cymbals on his knees.

- All: *Jersey Boys* will now end after the Big Three. But we will be running on the twenty-three show schedule.

- All: The five notes listed immediately above this one were actually co-written with other members of the JB: Toronto cast. Please judge them.

- All: Rick Elice says not to worry too much about being word-perfect. The lines are just an outline. Like good parents, they guide; they do not dictate.

- Knuckles: Please see me for an additional three-hundred-and-twelve pages of notes for you.

- All: Richard Hester has recommended we take fifteen minutes of running time off the show. Bob Crewe, two of your comic bits are cut. That should do it.

- All: A note from the Marketing Department…Company vehicles will be re-wired so that all honk-honk's will now be hoyt-hoyt's.

- Frankie: Line change…"So we hold auditions and find a couple of guys:

Nick Carter and A.J. McLean, both Backstreet Boys."

• All: Capitalizing on our strengths, we will now be selling *Jersey Boys* Swimsuit Calendars in the lobby. Francine, Mary, and Lorraine should each choose a month, and Bob Crewe will cover the remaining nine.

• Frankie: Please adjust your line to read, "Tommy was paying me twelve bucks a night when he was making a hundred and fifty. And he paid me in Canadian. So, really I was only making ten bucks a night USD gross, with the minimum fifteen percent non-resident withholding and taxable per diem, resulting in a ridiculous tax bill that April."

• All: The final moments of "Who Loves You" look terrific, but we need a little more action with those handheld six-inch mics. From now on, all Seasons should keep their right hand grasped firmly around their six-inch mics at all times. Nick should put his six-inch mic directly into Tommy's hands whenever possible. Bob, you should grab hold of whatever six-inch mics you can and gently rub them before showing your own six-inch mic to the audience. Frankie should dance around, waving his battery-powered six-inch mic and moving his mouth very close to Bob's six-inch mike (of course). Through all this, Tommy should mutter something about winter being cold and make a face like he's giving an excuse. (Note: Crewe will clean all six-inch mics after each performance.)

• All: Due to budget cuts, vocal doublers will now be telecommuting.

• Lorraine and Crewe: During "Silhouettes," we will now provide a shadow screen for you to actually create the silhouettes described in the song. (So hot.)

• Gyp: Instead of "My Mother's Eyes," please request that Frankie sing, "Pinball Wizard." (It was such a hit for Des in the 90s...)

• Frankie: After you say "running all over the map like a cockroach," please act it out.

• All: Allstate is now offering "Falling Down a Hole in the Stage When the Lift Fails" insurance with coverage for loss of limb and death.

• Frankie: When the cop tells you to make out your autograph to "Love Muffin," you should actually write "Low-Fat Blueberry Muffin." That will be wicked funny.

• All: Allstate's Risk Analysis Department has withdrawn its previous offer. No further information is available.

- Tommy: To help you with your opening speech, please place an emphasis on the second syllable of the word, "French."

- Frankie: "Fallen Angel" will now be replaced by the title song from "Grease." It is not as emotional, but it charted higher.

- Bob: When Finney at the record company asks, "What are you, busting my chops?" please respond with, "Yes, I am," then proceed to bust his chops big time.

- Frankie: In the tradition of John Lloyd, you must live like a monk to protect your voice. To promote this idea, you will now be required to make beer and jam for the rest of the cast on your day off.

- Knuckles: Eh. Never mind.

- All: We are missing an obvious opportunity. *Jersey Boys: Newark Company* will open next fall. The theatre will be next to a dump, next to a landfill, next to a liquor store, next to a five-floor walk-up, next to a rehab center, next to an off-track betting, next to...

- Hair Department: Please add a merkin. Anywhere. On anyone.

- Frankie: During your phone call when you hear Francine has died, we will now have Charlie Brown teacher sounds playing on the other end of the line.

- Tommy: Instead of "Tu stronzo disgraziato," please tell Frankie, "Voglio che tu dentro di me." ("I want you inside me.")

- All: A note from Music Supervisor Ron Melrose...Please make sure you articulate "Marianne" so people don't think you're saying "Mary Ann."

- Joey, Barry, Knuckles: During "Can't Take My Eyes Off of You," instead of playing a fake C# and F, please play a fake E and G#.

- All: Like Les Mis before it, *Jersey Boys Jr.* will premier at Long Island's Middletown Elementary School next fall.

- All: With *Jersey Boys Jr.*, we will need to make some script changes. All references to "wine" will be changed to "fruit punch," and all uses of the word "fuck" will be changed to "mother fuckin." (Because mothers will likely attend the performances.)

- All: If any Frankie gives you attitude, please refer to him as "Cranky."

- All: If any Frankie whines too much, please refer to him as "Francine."

- Bob and Crewe: When Frankie says, "It's like the Stations of the Cross," please present tableaus of the Stations of the Cross. Especially the one where Veronica wipes the face of Jesus and his face appears on the cloth. That's some freaky shit.

- French Rapper: Instead of "Ces Soir," you will now be singing "Pants on the Ground." It's a YouTube sensation.

- Knuckles: Good choices.

- Frankie: After you say, "You're right. I don't want to hear this," turn on your iPod and go home.

- Norm: New line…"You're moving to Vegas." "Vegas? For what?" "The new Wheel of Fortune slot machines at Harrah's." (I know this note isn't very funny, but have you ever tried those Wheel of Fortune slots? They are so fun, I had to give them a shout out.)

- All: Due to illness, each company will now have five swings, three universal swings, three non-performing understudies, four partial swings, and seventeen non-union covers.

- All: Previous note revoked. Producers are willing to take their chances.

- Frankie: In the first-date scene, instead of asking Mary, "So, this is a pretty nice place, huh?" please ask her, "So, have you read *Eat, Pray, Love?*" (And don't question this note. It will inspire her. Trust me.)

- Frankie: When Tommy points to Mary and says, "Hey Frankie, Type A," whatever you do, don't respond with, "But Tommy, Type A individuals are described as impatient, time-conscious, concerned about their status, highly competitive, ambitious, business-like, and aggressive individuals who have difficulty relaxing. They are often high-achieving workaholics who multi-task, drive themselves with deadlines, and are unhappy about delays." Quoting Wikipedia will never get you anywhere. Seriously.

- All: By now you are aware that *Jersey Boys* only allows one male and one female at a time to take vacation. To accommodate your special requests, the actor playing Joe Pesci will now be considered female under this rule, allowing Pesci and Tommy to vacation together forevermore.

- Norm Waxman: In honor of the latest Karate Kid remake, please Waxman on and Waxman off. Waxman on. Waxman off. Waxman on. Waxman off.

- Stage Management: From now on, Frankie's line "He couldn't help himself!" will be an acceptable excuse for anything related to the show.

210

Why was he late for half-hour? He couldn't help himself! Why did he miss his cue? He couldn't help himself! Why did he hit on the cougar that waited at the stage door? He couldn't help himself!

• Nick Massi: When playing fake bass, please add some fake dynamics. Add some fake volume at the top of "Sherry," then a fake slide down the fake octave during the fake chord changes at the top of "Big Girls."

• Nick: After Tommy says the bit about cheering for a team "that's from New York anyway," please check to make sure the audience gets the joke. If they don't get it, please help them out by whispering, "The Mets play in Jersey." Then act like you are wicked smart. (Get it?)

• Gyp: When you yell your line, "School kids!" can you please imagine The Four Seasons playing hopscotch on the playground? After you've imagined it, open your eyes and see what they've become. It'll be organic.

• All: If you do not hear enough piano in the monitor, kick the monitor.

• All: When you experience writer's block while creating funny *Jersey Boys* notes, please inform your readers so they will not judge them too harshly.

• All: When times get tough and cast sizes must be diminished, do not fear. Your costumes are expensive, so they will go on in your place.

• All: The House and Senate managed to pass a comprehensive health care bill, but it still won't include coverage for falling off the lip of the stage when a spotlight blinds your eyes.

• Tommy: When Norm tells you that you have to move to Vegas, please express a sigh of relief as you realize that they have *The Phantom of the Opera* there.

Thoughts? Comments? Dreams to share?

I would love to hear from you!

danielrobertsullivan@gmail.com

Iguana Books

iguanabooks.com

If you enjoyed *Places, Please!: Becoming a Jersey Boy*...

Look for other books coming soon from Iguana Books. Subscribe to our blog for updates as they happen.

iguanabooks.com/blog

You can also learn more about Daniel Robert Sullivan on his site.

danielrobertsullivan.iguanabooks.com

If you're a writer...

Iguana Books is always looking for great new writers, in every genre. We produce primarily ebooks but, as you can see, we do the occasional print book as well. Visit us at iguanabooks.com to see what Iguana Books has to offer both emerging and established authors.

iguanabooks.com/publishing-with-iguana/

If you're looking for another good book...

All Iguana books are available on our website. We pride ourselves on making sure that every Iguana book is a great read.

iguanabooks.com/bookstore/

Visit our bookstore today and support your favorite author.

CPSIA information can be obtained
at www.ICGtesting.com
Printed in the USA
FSOW04n0503020615
7497FS